Day Walks in Northumberland

20 coastal & countryside routes

Vertebrate Publishing, Sheffield
www.v-publishing.co.uk

Day Walks in Northumberland

20 coastal & countryside routes

David Wilson

Day Walks in Northumberland

20 coastal & countryside routes

VP First published in 2021 by **Vertebrate Publishing.** Reprinted in 2021.

Vertebrate Publishing, Omega Court, 352 Cemetery Road,
Sheffield S11 8FT, United Kingdom.
www.v-publishing.co.uk

Copyright © 2021 David Wilson and Vertebrate Publishing Ltd.

David Wilson has asserted his rights under the Copyright, Designs
and Patents Act 1988 to be identified as author of this work.

A CIP catalogue record for this book is available from the British Library.

ISBN 978-1-912560-61-5

All rights reserved. No part of this work covered by the copyright herein may be reproduced or used in any form or by any means — graphic, electronic, or mechanised, including photocopying, recording, taping, or information storage and retrieval systems – without the written permission of the publisher.

Front cover: View from Whitelaw Nick (route 9).
Back cover: Coble hut and Lindisfarne Castle (route 2).
Photography by **David Wilson** unless otherwise credited.

 All maps reproduced by permission of Ordnance Survey on behalf of The Controller of Her Majesty's Stationery Office.
© Crown Copyright. 100025218

Design by Nathan Ryder, production by Cameron Bonser.
www.**v-publishing**.co.uk

Printed and bound in Europe by Latitude Press.
Vertebrate Publishing is committed to printing on paper from sustainable sources.

MIX
Paper from responsible sources
FSC® C014138

Every effort has been made to achieve accuracy of the information in this guidebook. The authors, publishers and copyright owners can take no responsibility for: loss or injury (including fatal) to persons; loss or damage to property or equipment; trespass, irresponsible behaviour or any other mishap that may be suffered as a result of following the route descriptions or advice offered in this guidebook. The inclusion of a track or path as part of a route, or otherwise recommended, in this guidebook does not guarantee that the track or path will remain a right of way. If conflict with landowners arises we advise that you act politely and leave by the shortest route available. If the matter needs to be taken further then please take it up with the relevant authority.

Contents

Introduction	vii	Safety	x
Acknowledgements	viii	The Countryside Code	xi
About the walks	viii	How to use this book	xiv
Walk times	viii	Maps, descriptions, distances	xv
Navigation	viii	Km/mile conversion chart	xv
Long-distance trails	ix	Northumberland Area Map	xvi

SECTION 1 – NORTHUMBERLAND COAST

1. Coast & Castles – 22.1km/13.7miles … 5
2. The Holy Island of Lindisfarne – 17.2km/10.7miles … 13
3. Druridge Bay & River Coquet – 20.9km/13miles … 19

SECTION 2 – NORTHUMBERLAND NATIONAL PARK

4. Walltown & the Whin Sill – 17.7km/11miles … 29
5. Classic Hadrian's Wall Country – 12.7km/7.9miles … 35
6. Rothbury & Simonside Ridge – 12.9km/8miles … 41
7. Hedgehope Hill & Breamish Valley – 20.9km/13miles … 47
8. Ad Gefrin – 18.8km/11.7miles … 53
9. College Valley – 23.3km/14.5miles … 59
10. The Cheviot – 17.5km/10.9miles … 65
11. Barrowburn & the Border Ridge – 19.6km/12.2miles … 71
12. Border Reivers & Tarset Burn – 17.7km/11miles … 77

SECTION 3 – HISTORY & HERITAGE

13. Kielder Water North Shore – 22.5km/14miles … 87
14. Bolam Lake & Shaftoe Crags – 14km/8.7miles … 93
15. Alnwick Castle Estate – 13.5km/8.4miles … 99
16. Castles of the Tweed & Till – 23.2km/14.4miles … 103
17. Morpeth & River Wansbeck – 12.2km/7.6miles … 109
18. Allendale & Isaac's Tea Trail – 18.1km/11.2miles … 115
19. Thrunton Wood – 12.9km/8miles … 121
20. River South Tyne & Rails – 22.3km/13.9miles … 125

APPENDIX … 130

VIEW OVER THE COLLEGE VALLEY TOWARDS THE COAST

Introduction

My family's roots sit deep in the Northumberland landscape, from the coal mines in the south to the wilds of the north and the Cheviot Hills. This place has gifted me an appreciation of its natural wonders, and fired a passion to never stop exploring its rivers, valleys and hills. In 2016 I left the comfort of office life to pursue my passion for Northumberland and the great outdoors, and this book is the culmination of both the places I love to visit and the ones whose stories should be shared.

These routes offer the reader, and walker, the chance to explore a comprehensive selection of places which reflect Northumberland's natural, cultural and historical significance. Many places, such as the UNESCO World Heritage Site of Hadrian's Wall, will be familiar to many people, while others, such as the ancient settlement of Ad Gefrin, will offer new experiences, and memories to last a lifetime.

Northumberland is known as the 'land of the far horizon' and, from the miles of unspoilt coastline to the views from the great Whin Sill, and on to the undulating hills of the Cheviots, it's easy to see how it has earnt this title. The far-reaching views across river valleys and heather moorlands, forests and fields, bring into focus the many unique traits of this area. Northumberland has some of the cleanest rivers, the clearest air and, when night falls, the darkest skies – a unique place for body, mind and spirit.

The hidden charm to be found on these walks is something which cannot be put into words, or directions given to find. Traditional communities hold tightly on to their heritage to protect the legacy of what makes them great, and they proudly tell tales of ancestors who fished, mined, farmed and fought. There are castles which influenced Shakespeare, and locations straight out of Hollywood blockbusters, all visually stunning and all culturally priceless.

Northumberland has a proud history to be shared, and your journey from these pages to its paths make you part of that story forever.

David Wilson

Acknowledgements

Thanks to those that made this book possible. Emily Thompson – fellow Ordnance Survey Ambassador who suggested that I write this book. Ordnance Survey – who have supported me as a GetOutside Champion since 2017. Jack Wilson – my twelve-year-old son who joined me on some of the walks. And finally, Rhoda Wilson – my Gran, who sadly passed away the week before I finished this book. She made me walk everywhere as a child, which proved to be good preparation for this great writing adventure.

About the walks

The walks featured in this book are split into three sections: Northumberland Coast, Northumberland National Park and History & Heritage. They vary in distance from 12.2 to 23.3 kilometres (7.6 to 14.5 miles) and offer a comprehensive range of walking from routes starting and finishing in towns, to routes in some of the remotest places in England.

Walk times

All of the walks listed have an estimated time in the summary. These times are based on a walking speed of four kilometres per hour and, where appropriate, some added time for brief rest stops. Most of the walks feature a place of interest, and you should plan accordingly for these when deciding how long a walk will take to complete.

Navigation

Northumberland is covered in full by a number of Ordnance Survey (OS) Explorer 1:25,000 or OS Landranger 1:50,000 maps. While the route descriptions and maps provided in this book give detailed information on the walks, it is important to have a basic understanding of navigation. It is always useful to take a separate map on your walk, along with a compass.

The routes in this book are covered by the following maps in the OS 1:25,000 Explorer series:

- OL16 The Cheviot Hills
- OL42 Kielder Water & Forest
- OL43 Hadrian's Wall
- 325 Morpeth & Blyth
- 332 Alnwick & Amble
- 339 Kelso, Coldstream & Lower Tweed Valley
- 340 Holy Island & Bamburgh

Long-distance trails

The following long-distance trails – both local and national – feature on some of the walking routes in this book. These trails are waymarked and can be found on the appropriate OS maps, with further details available online.

» **Hadrian's Wall Path** (see routes 4 and 5) – 84-mile trail from coast to coast following the iconic UNESCO World Heritage Site of Hadrian's Wall.
   www.nationaltrail.co.uk/hadrians-wall-path
» **Isaac's Tea Trail** (see route 18) – 36-mile circular trail exploring the route of tea seller Isaac Holden on his journey in the North Pennines. It is England's last great undiscovered wilderness trek. www.isaacs-tea-trail.co.uk
» **Northumberland Coast Path** (see routes 1 and 3) – 62 miles of some of the best coastal walking in Europe. This trail explores the rich and varied coastline of England's border county. www.northumberlandcoastpath.org
» **Pennine Way** (see routes 4, 5, 9, 10, 11 and 20) – 268-mile trail along the backbone of England from Edale to Kirk Yetholm. www.nationaltrail.co.uk/pennine-way
» **River Tyne Trail** (see routes 12, 13 and 20) – 135-mile trail following the River Tyne from its northern source in Northumberland and its southern source in Cumbria, to its end at the North Sea. www.daftasabrush.org.uk/river-tyne-trail
» **South Tyne Trail** (see route 20) – 23-mile trail running from the source of the River South Tyne near Garrigill to Haltwhistle. www.northpennines.org.uk/location/south-tyne-trail
» **St Cuthbert's Way** (see routes 2, 8 and 9) – 62 miles of history and culture stretching from Melrose in the Scottish Borders to Holy Island in Northumberland.
   www.stcuthbertsway.info
» **St Oswald's Way** (see routes 1, 2, 3 and 6) – 97 miles of historic Northumberland landscapes linking the places associated with St Oswald, King of Northumbria.
   www.stoswaldsway.com

Safety

Before beginning any of these walks it is important to ensure you are fully prepared for changeable conditions both in terms of weather and underfoot. Having the correct clothing and equipment is crucial, and you should always be fully prepared for any adverse or emergency situations.

A number of these walks encounter a variety of hazards from busy roads to fields of livestock. *The Ramblers* have a good online resource with safety information for walkers: **www.ramblers.org.uk/advice/safety**

In respect to navigation, consider downloading OS Locate from Ordnance Survey. This is an app which allows you to quickly and accurately pinpoint your location for reassurance or rescue.

Rescue

In case of an emergency dial **999** and ask for **Police** and then **Mountain Rescue**. Where possible give a six-figure grid reference of your location or that of your casualty. If you don't have mobile reception try to attract the attention of others nearby. The standard distress signal is six short blasts on a whistle every minute.

Emergency rescue by SMS text

In the UK you can also contact the emergency services by SMS text – useful if you have low battery or intermittent signal. You need to register your phone first by texting **'register'** to **999** and then following the instructions in the reply. **Do it now** – it could save yours or someone else's life. **www.emergencysms.net**

The Countryside Code

Respect other people
Please respect the local community and other people using the outdoors. Remember your actions can affect people's lives and livelihoods.

Consider the local community and other people enjoying the outdoors
» Respect the needs of local people and visitors alike – for example, don't block gateways, driveways or other paths with your vehicle.
» When riding a bike or driving a vehicle, slow down or stop for horses, walkers and farm animals and give them plenty of room. By law, cyclists must give way to walkers and horse riders on bridleways.
» Co-operate with people at work in the countryside. For example, keep out of the way when farm animals are being gathered or moved and follow directions from the farmer.
» Busy traffic on small country roads can be unpleasant and dangerous to local people, visitors and wildlife – so slow down and where possible, leave your vehicle at home, consider sharing lifts and use alternatives such as public transport or cycling. For public transport information, phone Traveline on 0871 200 22 33 or visit **www.traveline.info**

Leave gates and property as you find them and follow paths unless wider access is available
» A farmer will normally close gates to keep farm animals in, but may sometimes leave them open so the animals can reach food and water. Leave gates as you find them or follow instructions on signs. When in a group, make sure the last person knows how to leave the gates.
» Follow paths unless wider access is available, such as on open country or registered common land (known as 'open access land').
» If you think a sign is illegal or misleading such as a *Private – No Entry* sign on a public path, contact the local authority.
» Leave machinery and farm animals alone – don't interfere with animals even if you think they're in distress. Try to alert the farmer instead.
» Use gates, stiles or gaps in field boundaries if you can – climbing over walls, hedges and fences can damage them and increase the risk of farm animals escaping.
» Our heritage matters to all of us – be careful not to disturb ruins and historic sites.

Protect the natural environment

We all have a responsibility to protect the countryside now and for future generations, so make sure you don't harm animals, birds, plants or trees and try to leave no trace of your visit. When out with your dog make sure it is not a danger or nuisance to farm animals, horses, wildlife or other people.

Leave no trace of your visit and take your litter home

- Protecting the natural environment means taking special care not to damage, destroy or remove features such as rocks, plants and trees. They provide homes and food for wildlife, and add to everybody's enjoyment of the countryside.
- Litter and leftover food doesn't just spoil the beauty of the countryside, it can be dangerous to wildlife and farm animals – so take your litter home with you. Dropping litter and dumping rubbish are criminal offences.
- Fires can be as devastating to wildlife and habitats as they are to people and property – so be careful with naked flames and cigarettes at any time of the year. Sometimes, controlled fires are used to manage vegetation, particularly on heaths and moors between 1 October and 15 April, but if a fire appears to be unattended then report it by calling **999**.

Keep dogs under effective control

When you take your dog into the outdoors, always ensure it does not disturb wildlife, farm animals, horses or other people by keeping it under effective control. This means that you:
- keep your dog on a lead, or
- keep it in sight at all times, be aware of what it's doing and be confident it will return to you promptly on command
- ensure it does not stray off the path or area where you have a right of access

Special dog rules may apply in particular situations, so always look out for local signs – for example:
- dogs may be banned from certain areas that people use, or there may be restrictions, byelaws or control orders limiting where they can go
- the access rights that normally apply to open country and registered common land (known as 'open access' land) require dogs to be kept on a short lead between 1 March and 31 July, to help protect ground nesting birds, and all year round near farm animals

» at the coast, there may also be some local restrictions to require dogs to be kept on a short lead during the bird breeding season, and to prevent disturbance to flocks of resting and feeding birds during other times of year

It's always good practice (and a legal requirement on 'open access' land) to keep your dog on a lead around farm animals and horses, for your own safety and for the welfare of the animals. A farmer may shoot a dog which is attacking or chasing farm animals without being liable to compensate the dog's owner.

However, if cattle or horses chase you and your dog, it is safer to let your dog off the lead – don't risk getting hurt by trying to protect it. Your dog will be much safer if you let it run away from a farm animal in these circumstances and so will you.

Everyone knows how unpleasant dog mess is and it can cause infections, so always clean up after your dog and get rid of the mess responsibly – 'bag it and bin it'. Make sure your dog is wormed regularly to protect it, other animals and people.

Enjoy the outdoors

Even when going out locally, it's best to get the latest information about where and when you can go. For example, your rights to go onto some areas of open access land and coastal land may be restricted in particular places at particular times. Find out as much as you can about where you are going, plan ahead and follow advice and local signs.

Plan ahead and be prepared

You'll get more from your visit if you refer to up-to-date maps or guidebooks and websites before you go. Visit **www.gov.uk/natural-england** or contact local information centres or libraries for a list of outdoor recreation groups offering advice on specialist activities.

You're responsible for your own safety and for others in your care – especially children – so be prepared for natural hazards, changes in weather and other events. Wild animals, farm animals and horses can behave unpredictably if you get too close, especially if they're with their young – so give them plenty of space.

Check weather forecasts before you leave. Conditions can change rapidly especially on mountains and along the coast, so don't be afraid to turn back. When visiting the coast check for tide times on **www.ukho.gov.uk/easytide** – don't risk getting cut off by rising tides and take care on slippery rocks and seaweed.

Part of the appeal of the countryside is that you can get away from it all. You may not see anyone for hours, and there are many places without clear mobile phone signals, so let someone else know where you're going and when you expect to return.

Follow advice and local signs
England has about 190,000km (118,000 miles) of public rights of way, providing many opportunities to enjoy the natural environment. Get to know the signs and symbols used in the countryside to show paths and open countryside.

How to use this book

This book should provide you with all the information you need for an enjoyable, trouble-free and successful walk. The following tips should help:

1. We strongly recommend that you invest in the relevant OS map for the walk (see page viii) in case you need to cut short the walk or take an alternative route.

2. Choose your route carefully taking into account the time available, abilities and experience of all those in your group and weather forecast – read the safety section of this guidebook.

3. We recommend that you study the route description carefully before setting off. Cross-reference this with your map so that you've got a good sense of general orientation in case you need an escape route. Make sure that you are familiar with the symbols used on the maps.

4. Get out there and get walking!

Maps, descriptions, distances

While every effort has been made to maintain accuracy within the maps and descriptions in this guidebook, we have had to process a vast amount of information and we are unable to guarantee that every single detail is correct. Please exercise caution if a direction appears at odds with the route on the map. If in doubt, a comparison between the route, the description and a quick cross-reference with your map (along with a bit of common sense) should help ensure that you're on the right track.

Note that distances have been measured off the map, and map distances rarely coincide 100 per cent with distances on the ground. Please treat stated distances as a guideline only. Ordnance Survey maps are the most commonly used, are easy to read and many people are happy using them. If you're not familiar with OS maps and are unsure of what the symbols mean, you can download a free OS 1:25,000 map legend from **www.ordnancesurvey.co.uk**

Here are a few of the symbols and abbreviations we use on the maps and in our directions:

 ROUTE STARTING POINT    ROUTE MARKER    SHORTCUT

 OPTIONAL ROUTE    ADDITIONAL GRID LINE NUMBERS TO AID NAVIGATION

Km/mile conversion chart

Metric to Imperial

1 kilometre [km]	1,000 m	0.6214 mile
1 metre [m]	100 cm	1.0936 yd
1 centimetre [cm]	10 mm	0.3937 in
1 millimetre [mm]		0.03937 in

Imperial to Metric

1 mile	1,760 yd	1.6093 km
1 yard [yd]	3 ft	0.9144 m
1 foot [ft]	12 in	0.3048 m
1 inch [in]		2.54 cm

#	Walk	Page
1	Coast & Castles	5
2	The Holy Island of Lindisfarne	13
3	Druridge Bay & River Coquet	19
4	Walltown & the Whin Sill	29
5	Classic Hadrian's Wall Country	35
6	Rothbury & Simonside Ridge	41
7	Hedgehope Hill & Breamish Valley	47
8	Ad Gefrin	53
9	College Valley	59
10	The Cheviot	65
11	Barrowburn & the Border Ridge	71
12	Border Reivers & Tarset Burn	77
13	Kielder Water North Shore	87
14	Bolam Lake & Shaftoe Crags	93
15	Alnwick Castle Estate	99
16	Castles of the Tweed & Till	103
17	Morpeth & River Wansbeck	109
18	Allendale & Isaac's Tea Trail	115
19	Thrunton Wood	121
20	River South Tyne & Rails	125

DAY WALKS IN NORTHUMBERLAND

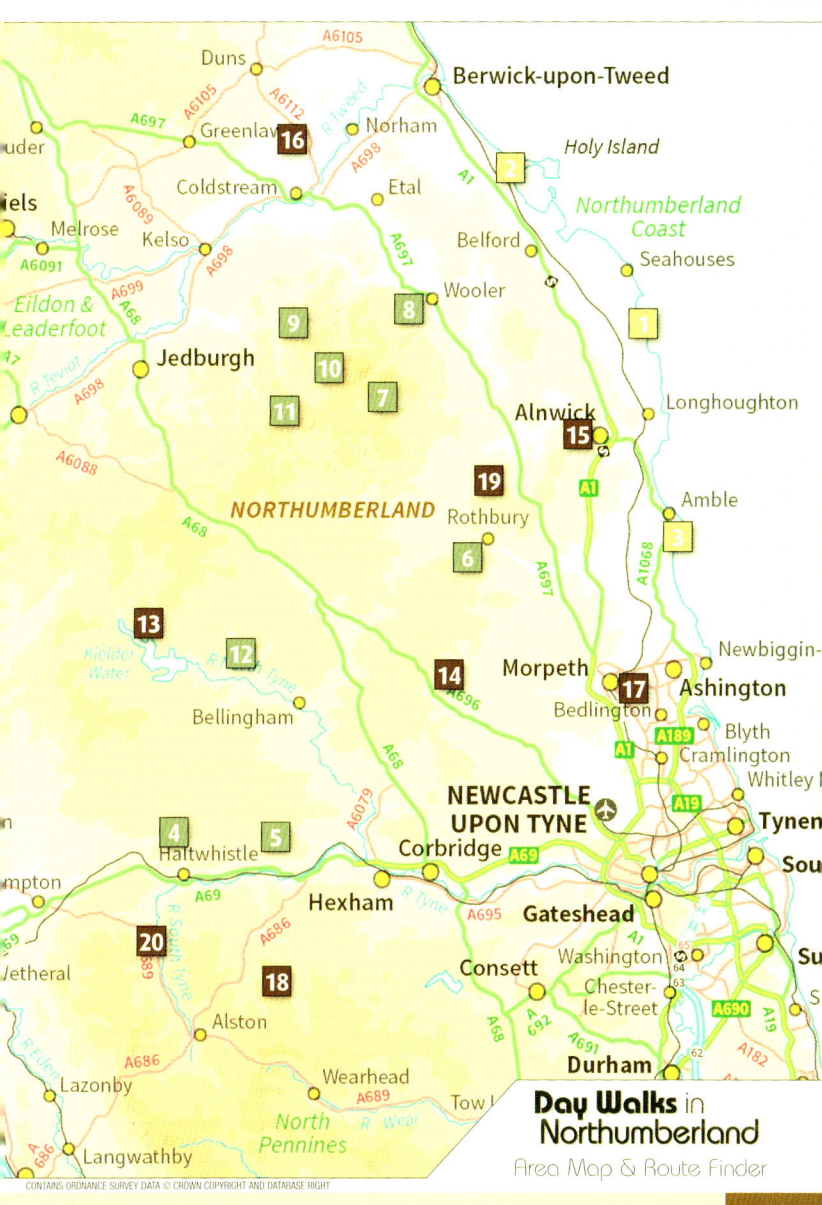

SECTION 1

Northumberland Coast

The Northumberland Coast is one of England's hidden gems with 40 miles of it being designated as an Area of Outstanding Natural Beauty. A journey along the shoreline visits beaches guarded by castles, traditional fishing villages alongside seaside towns, and nature reserves protecting some of the country's most important wildlife.

A walk along this unique coastline gives memories to last a lifetime.

BEADNELL HARBOUR

BAMBURGH CASTLE FROM THE BEACH. PHOTO: KEVIN EAVES/SHUTTERSTOCK.COM

LOW NEWTON-BY-THE-SEA

01 Coast & Castles

22.1km/13.7miles

A linear route visiting some must-see spots along the Northumberland Coast. From quiet fishing villages to popular seaside towns, this walk has coastline, castles and lots of Northumbrian culture.

Craster » Dunstanburgh Castle » Embleton Bay » Low Newton-by-the-Sea » Beadnell » Seahouses » Bamburgh Castle

Start
Craster car park (parking charge).
GR: NU 256198.

The Walk
This route is most enjoyed when walked on the beach, giving unbroken views along the coast with sand between your toes. There's no better place to be on Northumberland's shores. The route also features two long-distance trails: the Northumberland Coast Path and St Oswald's Way.

Starting in the fishing village of Craster, home of the famous Craster Kippers and smokehouse for over 100 years, the trail sets off across the National Trust reserve towards Dunstanburgh Castle. Grass track is watched over by the fourteenth-century fortress – this section is one of the finest walks on the east coast.

Beyond the castle, the trail goes past a World War II pillbox and on to the beach. The walk along Embleton Bay offers views back to Dunstanburgh Castle and Castle Point crags and ahead to the carrs surrounding Newton Haven. Upon arriving at Low Newton-by-the-Sea a warm welcome awaits from the whitewashed buildings of this picturesque coastal hamlet. A must visit is the eighteenth-century pub, The Ship Inn. A walk across the dunes of Newton Links leads to the Long Nanny bird reserve next to the burn of the same name. A bridge crosses the burn to keep feet dry. Ahead is Beadnell Harbour and its eighteenth-century lime kilns.

The penultimate town on the route is a popular seaside haven with a rich fishing heritage: Seahouses now boasts a fleet of boats taking visitors to the Farne Islands.

Leaving Seahouses, the horizon is now dominated by the mighty fortress of Bamburgh Castle. Bamburgh was the ancient capital of the kingdom of Northumbria, and a fitting end to a day's walk.

COAST & CASTLES

DISTANCE: 22.1KM/13.7MILES » **TOTAL ASCENT:** 225M/738FT » **START GR:** NU 256198 » **TIME:** ALLOW 6.5 HOURS (EXCLUDING 45-MINUTE RETURN BUS JOURNEY) » **SATNAV:** NE66 3TW » **MAP:** OS EXPLORER 332, ALNWICK & AMBLE, AND 340, HOLY ISLAND & BAMBURGH, 1:25,000 » **REFRESHMENTS:** THE JOLLY FISHERMAN, CRASTER; THE SHIP INN, LOW NEWTON-BY-THE-SEA; THE BAMBURGH CASTLE INN, SEAHOUSES; THE CASTLE INN, BAMBURGH **NAVIGATION:** STRAIGHTFORWARD – FOLLOWING BEACH OR DUNE PATHS.

01 COAST & CASTLES – NORTHUMBERLAND COAST

Directions – Coast & Castles

❺▸ Leave the car park and **turn right** into the village. At the harbour take the **first left turn** signed *Coastal Path to Dunstanburgh*. Follow this path along the coastline through various gates and eventually meet a track leading up a small embankment. Stay on the coastline – **don't take the left-hand track** – and follow the path uphill and towards Dunstanburgh Castle. **Walk towards the gatehouse.**

2 **Walk to the left of castle,** along its fence line; the path drops down below the towers. After the final tower the track bears left to a kissing gate signed for *Dunstanburgh Golf Club* and *St Oswald's Way* – to the right are views of the crags at Castle Point. Once through the gates **stay on the right-hand track** – don't take the golf club trail – and continue along the dunes. Pass the World War II pillbox on your left and, as views open up along the coast, **turn right along a track down through dunes on to the beach.** Walk for 800m along the beach* and, to keep feet dry, **turn left** up into dunes. Follow the trail over a footbridge and **turn right** to cross The Skaith stream; once clear of the stream rejoin the beach.

> * Happy to de-shoe? Continue straight ahead and through the outlet of The Skaith stream.

At this point **walk along beach for approximately 1.3km** to reach Low Newton-by-the-Sea. Public toilets are located behind The Ship Inn – around the right-hand side of the buildings.

3 **Walk up the road for 50m then turn right,** signed *National Trust Newton Point & Beadnell 2½*. Follow the path (St Oswald's Way/Northumberland Coast Path) which leads along the back of dunes, **through a car park**, and onwards to a footbridge over the Long Nanny burn. After the burn **turn right to** return to the beach and **walk all the way to Beadnell Harbour**. Approach the **harbour from its left-hand side** and take the steps up on to the harbour walls and lime kilns. Follow the road from the lime kilns all the way through the village and begin to get views of the Farne Islands. **Pass a shop and picnic area** then, at a road junction, **turn right through a gate** and join the beach.

01 COAST & CASTLES CONTINUED

Directions – Coast & Castles continued...

4 Turn left along the beach and **walk for approximately 1.8km.** As you approach the cliff, **turn left into the dunes** and towards a group of World War II anti-tank blocks. At the blocks follow close to the cliff along rocks for 150m then **turn left up to the golf course. Follow black footpath posts** across the golf course, staying next to the coastline. With the harbour visible ahead go through a kissing gate. **After a caravan park follow a sign for** *Coast Path* in front of houses and down to Harbour Road and North Sunderland Harbour.

5 From the harbour (next to the boat trip huts) **walk past the RNLI building on your right** to the main road (public toilets and the town centre are to the left). **Turn right** and walk along the road, then **bear right** on to the roadside path which heads down to the beach. Follow the beach, with views out to the Farne Islands, until you reach Clashope Burn. **Turn left up to Monks House** and cross the small burn next to the property before returning to the beach. Continue ahead with views of Bamburgh Castle up ahead, and Lindisfarne Castle out to sea. **Walk past Bamburgh Castle towers** to where dunes open revealing a footpath. **Follow the footpath in the dunes,** on the right-hand side of the castle, and at a *Village* sign **turn right.** The path leads to the other side of the castle and village green. **Cross the field to the corner and exit on to the main road** next to the bus stop opposite the Lord Crewe Hotel. The return journey (approximately 45 minutes) to Craster village is via Arriva buses with the most frequent service being the X18.

LINDISFARNE PRIORY WITH LINDISFARNE CASTLE

02 The Holy Island of Lindisfarne 17.2km/10.7miles

Walk in the footsteps of saints on a journey first travelled in AD635 by St Aidan. This unique island experience takes you across the Pilgrim's Way, offering the walk of a lifetime.

Beal End car park » Pilgrim's Way » St Cuthbert's Isle » Village Green » Lindisfarne Castle » The Lough » The Links » Village Green » Pilgrim's Way » Beal End car park

Start
Beal End car park (small car park), 1.2km east of The Barn at Beal. GR: NU 079427.

The Walk
A unique and memorable walk, but one that comes with words of caution: **check tide and crossing times carefully.**

To complete this walk, and enjoy Lindisfarne fully, you must ensure there is ample time to get back across the causeway at the end of your walk (total walk is five hours and thirty minutes giving time for refreshments). Before completing this walk ensure you have a minimum of six hours of **safe crossing time** available by checking the Holy Island crossing times online. This walk is most enjoyed barefoot as it crosses shallow water and some sections of clay and mud.

Lindisfarne was founded in AD635 when St Aidan travelled to Lindisfarne at the request of King Oswald – his mission was to bring Christianity to the people of Northumbria. Upon Aidan's death, St Cuthbert saw a vision of his destiny and walked to Holy Island, from Melrose, to eventually become Bishop of Lindisfarne.

Both men walked the route across the sands to seek the sanctity of the island, making it a popular pilgrimage route now for worshippers. Upon reaching Lindisfarne, the first stopping point on this walk is St Cuthbert's Isle, where he briefly retired to for peaceful prayer before leaving for his final resting place on the Farne Islands.

A century after Cuthbert, the island gained some unwelcome visitors in the form of Vikings, and this ultimately led to the inhabitants fleeing for the safety of the mainland.

When people returned to the island it began a timeline which saw new religious settlements, defensive fortifications and eventually a small community built on traditional industries and a unique way of life.

THE HOLY ISLAND OF LINDISFARNE

DISTANCE: 17.2KM/10.7MILES » **TOTAL ASCENT:** 68M/223FT » **START GR:** NU 079427 » **TIME:** ALLOW 5.5 HOURS
SATNAV: TD15 2PB » **MAP:** OS EXPLORER 340, HOLY ISLAND & BAMBURGH, 1:25,000 » **REFRESHMENTS:** THE BARN AT BEAL (1.3KM WEST OF THE STARTING POINT) OR A CHOICE OF PUBS AND CAFES ON THE ISLAND
NAVIGATION: STRAIGHTFORWARD – CHECK SAFE CROSSING TIMES.

Directions – The Holy Island of Lindisfarne

S ▶ **This section should take a maximum of 1 hour and 30 minutes.** From the car park **turn left** and walk along the road towards the Refuge Box. The start of the wooden posts marking the Pilgrim's Way can be seen on the right. **Stay on the road over the bridge** and pass the Refuge Box. **Turn right on to the sand** and make your way across to the wooden post line and follow the posts across the causeway. Pass another Refuge Box and continue following the post line. Around 20 or 30 minutes after the second Refuge Box listen for the sound of the seals on the sand bank to the right towards the Old Law Beacons at Guile Point. Continue until you reach the island.

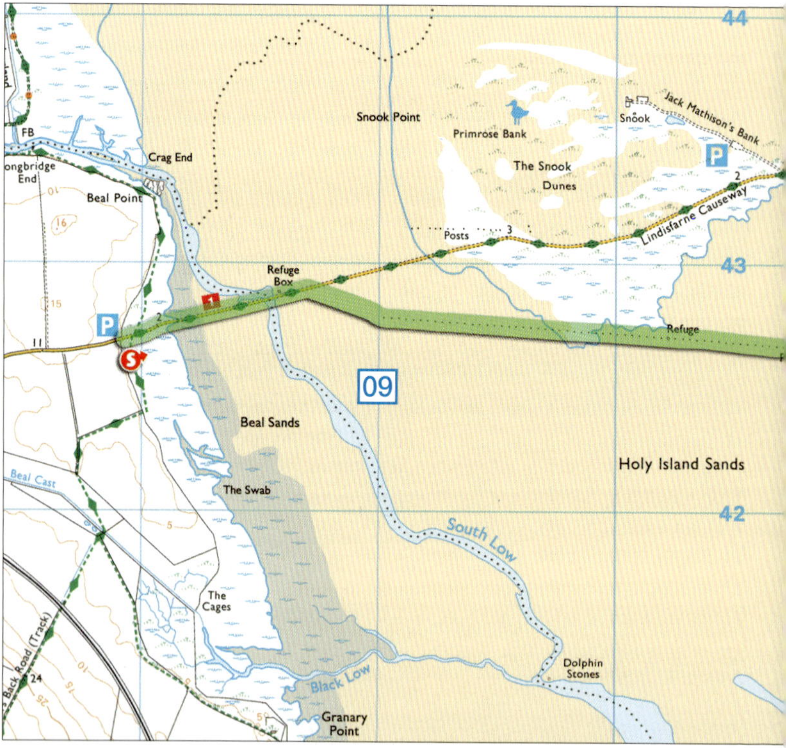

2 The Island walk will take around 2 hours and 30 minutes. **Turn right** at the information board **and walk along the shore**. Continue to follow the dune and rock shoreline all the way around to St Cuthbert's Isle (off to the right). Visit the island and then **return towards the old lifeboat station** – now a heritage centre. Follow the path to the back of the building on to the Public Footpath and **turn right** heading towards the church. At the road **go straight across to enter the churchyard**. Leave via the path to the English Heritage Lindisfarne Priory Museum after exploring the church area.

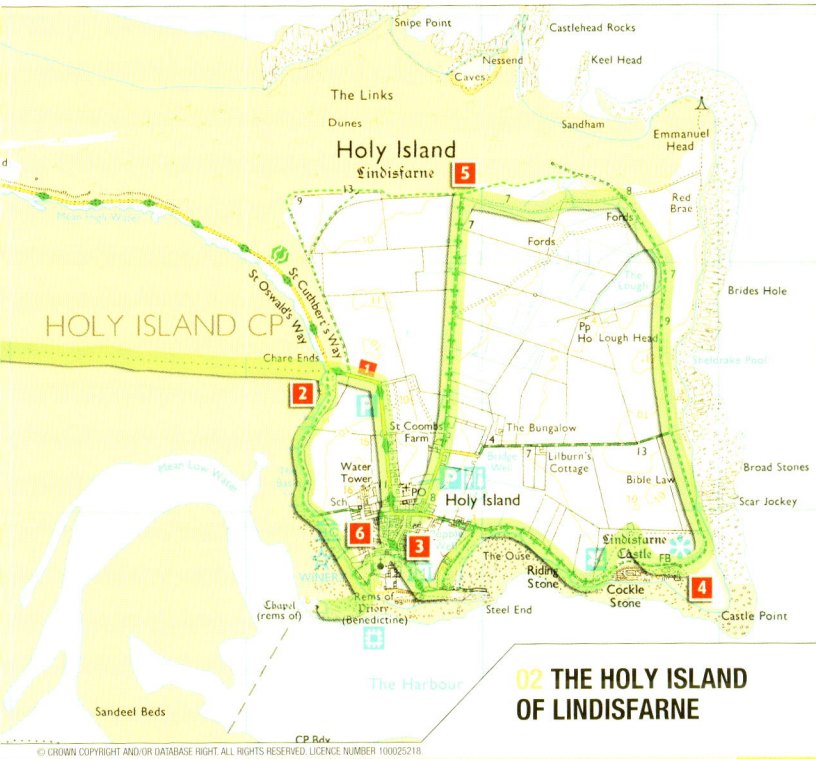

02 THE HOLY ISLAND OF LINDISFARNE

Directions – The Holy Island of Lindisfarne continued...

3 Go past the museum and **turn right at village green** and go towards the Crown & Anchor Inn. **At the right-hand side** of the pub is a path marked *Public Footpath*; walk along this path to a gate/turnstile and then **turn left towards fishing huts**. Upon reaching the fishing 'village' **turn left** and follow a track past coble sheds (upturned boats) to reach the road. **Turn right and follow the road towards Lindisfarne Castle.** Go through a kissing gate; after 20m **turn left across the field to a walled garden** (Gertrude Jekyll garden). After exploring the garden head back towards the castle on the **track which heads to the left of the castle**. Take steps up to the castle (on the right is the entrance to the National Trust site); **turn left** and, with the castle behind you, **take the path on the right** down to the front of the lime kilns.

4 **Continue straight ahead from the lime kilns then turn left on to a track** which follows the coastline and goes through an opening in a wall. The path passes a fingerpost pointing to a bird hide, then the path passes The Lough on your left. Reach a stile and continue straight ahead to a gate next to dunes. **Turn left and follow a wall** (on your left). Walk until reach Lindisfarne National Nature Reserve sign number 8.

5 **Turn left and follow the path back into the village**. Continue through a farm, on to a road, and straight ahead into the village along Sandham Lane. **Turn right** along Marygate then, just past The Ship Inn, **turn left** to reach the village green again.

6 To leave the village head away from the village green **towards Lindisfarne Mead**, passing public toilets on the left. At the road junction **turn right and then left** and walk past the public car park and back down to the start of the causeway crossing. At this point you can follow the road all the way across the causeway back to the start, or take the Pilgrim's Way again. The Pilgrim's Way is around 500m shorter than the road but is slower due to terrain. **The route across the sand will take around 1 hour and 30 minutes.**

HOLY ISLAND VILLAGE

AMBLE PIER

03 Druridge Bay & River Coquet   20.9km/13miles

A coast and country circular, taking in the beautiful beach of Druridge Bay and visiting the River Coquet settlements of Amble and Warkworth.

Druridge Bay Country Park » Druridge Bay » Hauxley Nature Reserve » Amble » Warkworth » St Oswald's Way » Togston » Druridge Bay Country Park

Start
Druridge Bay Country Park visitor centre car park (parking charge). GR: NZ 272998.

The Walk
The walk leaves a former opencast coalmine, now a country park, to join one of Northumberland's most popular beaches. Druridge Bay has amazing views along its eleven-kilometre stretch, and its neighbouring nature reserves make it a wildlife haven.

The coal mining heritage of this area comes from rich coal deposits laid down millions of years ago, when the area was forest and swamp. Evidence of this geology is visible on rejoining the beach beyond Low Hauxley. Under dunes, but exposed on the sand by erosion, there's a black seam of fascinating fossilised forest.

The next port of call is Amble. A traditional and now modernised harbour village welcomes visitors in what is known as the 'friendliest port in England', a reference to a 1930s telegram from *RMS Mauretania* as it passed.

Along the River Coquet, with views of its castle ahead, is the historic town of Warkworth. A town with many unique features, this is a significant place in Northumbrian history. From its rebel baron who secured the Magna Carta in 1215 (see St Lawrence Church), to the thirteenth-century burgage plots leading to the only remaining fortified bridge in England.

Warkworth's highlight, and sitting at the top of the village, is its twelfth-century castle. A Percy family castle (see route 15), this is one of Northumberland's finest unadulterated fortifications.

Leaving Warkworth, and briefly joining St Oswald's Way, the return leg goes through the village of Togston before returning to Druridge and the chance to enjoy the country park.

DRURIDGE BAY & RIVER COQUET

DISTANCE: 20.9KM/13MILES » **TOTAL ASCENT:** 151M/495FT » **START GR:** NZ 272998 » **TIME:** ALLOW 6 HOURS
SATNAV: NE61 5BX » **MAP:** OS EXPLORER 325, MORPETH & BLYTH, AND 332, ALNWICK & AMBLE, 1:25,000
REFRESHMENTS: DRURIDGE BAY COUNTRY PARK CAFE; VARIOUS OPTIONS IN AMBLE AND WARKWORTH
NAVIGATION: STRAIGHTFORWARD.

03 DRURIDGE BAY & RIVER COQUET

Directions – Druridge Bay & River Coquet

➎ Leave the car park and **follow signs for** *Beach*, crossing the road and taking a path through trees to a wooden walkway. **Turn left** passing the World War II anti-tank blocks along the dunes. Follow the beach for 2.2km until you reach a sign on the left for *Togston Links car park*. **Leave the beach here.**

2 **Turn right and walk along the road**, which turns into a path. Pass a sign for *Hauxley Wildlife Discovery Centre 1km* and continue along the path. **Turn left** at a signed path junction towards the Discovery Centre. (If you don't want to visit continue straight ahead.) After visiting the Discovery Centre **retrace your steps** to the signed path junction and **turn left** (signed *Amble 3.5km*). After a short distance reach Low Hauxley, **walk all the way through houses** (following *England Coast Path* signs). Before the car park **turn right through dunes on to the beach,** where you can see the remains of a fossilised forest and views of Coquet Island. Continue along the beach. Before the end of beach, **leave on the left via steps and a boardwalk,** through dunes to meet a track. **Bear right** along the track and pass a caravan park. Continue to follow *England Coast Path* signs to the rear of dunes and past a playground. The path leads on to **Amble's South Jetty**. Follow the jetty round to the harbour.

3 Walk through the modern harbour shops, and past the Northumberland Seafood Centre. **Turn right at the main road** and continue through the town centre via Queen Street. **Turn right on to North Street** – signed *Marina & Braid* – to meet a gravel track alongside the boat yard. The path then meets the River Coquet heading to Warkworth with views of Warkworth Castle ahead. Follow the path alongside the road all the way into Warkworth to meet a T-junction.

4 **Turn right at the junction** and walk along the road towards the castle. **Fork right** on to Castle Terrace; walk past the Sun Hotel then **take the small path to the right of Roxbro House** – signed *Warkworth Br ¼*. The path leads between burgage plots to reach the road and medieval bridge. **Follow the path to the left of the bridge** – signed *Monks Walk/Coast Path*. **Turn left after the church** to meet the main street. Stay on the right-hand side of the road heading for the castle.

5 Now on St Oswald's Way, **enter the castle grounds** at the top of the street and walk to the right-hand side of the castle. The path follows steps up to a car park and public toilets (open during castle opening hours). **Walk past the toilets on your right and follow the left-hand track to the main road.** Cross the road, **turn right then immediately left** – signed *Togston & Broomhill*. **Turn right on to Warkworth Avenue** (signed *St Oswald's Way*) and then **turn left on to a track.** Follow the track for 1.7km then at a signpost follow sign for *Togston 1*, leaving St Oswald's Way. **After 750m and before the track goes through a gate, turn left on to a grass trail through trees.** Keep straight ahead until you reach a hedge then **turn left on to a path into Togston.**

6 **Turn left at the main road**, pass a bus stop and **turn right on to Queen Street** to follow a path around the rear of gardens and allotments. As track bears to the right follow it for 10m and then **enter a field straight ahead. Turn left** to follow the field border (with trees on your left) for four fields. At the corner of field/wooded area – signed *Public Footpath* – enter the trees (this path can be overgrown but is passable). Follow the path to copse edge, **turn right and look out for stile** to cross into the next field. On **entering the field turn right** and follow the treeline (on your right) all the way around to main road and take the track bending around to the subway.

7 Leave the subway and at road level turn right on to a track signed *Public Footpath*. The path leads to a Druridge Bay Country Park gate, **turn right here and follow signs for** *Lakeshore Walk*. After 450m **turn left down a track to a weir** and stepping stones. **Cross the stepping stones and turn left.** Follow the path along the lakeside all the way back to the start.

SECTION 2

Northumberland National Park

Northumberland National Park is the most northerly national park in England with the lowest population density of any of the national parks. It stretches from the Scottish Borders down to Hadrian's Wall, with the undulating hills of the Cheviots at its heart. A land of remote landscapes and wild beauty, it offers a rich history and heritage from the Romans to the railways of the Industrial Revolution.

MILECASTLE 42

04 Walltown & the Whin Sill   17.7km/11miles

A walk to experience the geography, geology and history of Hadrian's Wall – from the great Whin Sill that the wall stands on, to the castles built from the wall's stone.

Walltown » Thirlwall Castle » Moss Peteral » Cawfields Quarry » Aesica Roman Fort » Walltown Crags » Walltown

Start
Walltown Visitor Centre, Greenhead (parking charge). GR: NY 668658.

The Walk
Hadrian's Wall has been a prominent feature of the Northumberland landscape for nearly 2,000 years. Built as the northern frontier of the Roman Empire, the wall highlights both the beauty of this landscape and the ingenuity of the Romans.

Walltown is a perfect base for this walk, with a visitor centre sitting under dramatic wall-topped crags. Walking out of Walltown there are numerous examples of how the Romans did more than just 'build a wall', such as where the path leads along a section of Vallum – a defensive ditch which was dug south of the wall across the country. While the wall provided defence for around 300 years during Roman times, it subsequently provided stone for many of Northumberland's other defensive structures, including the fourteenth-century Thirlwall Castle.

Beyond the castle is Thirlwall Common and Moss Peteral. A landscape of meadows, moorlands and wetlands where those that visit see the rarely enjoyed southerly views to the wall. The north side of the Whin Sill crag exposes the volcanic rock face which is crowned by the wall, a true testament to Roman engineering.

Cawfields Quarry closed in 1944, and highlights the industrial impact on heritage sites such as Hadrian's Wall, while now offering a peaceful natural resting spot. Take the time to explore Milecastle 42, then climb to the top of the crag and view the line of Vallum below.

Heading back to Walltown, the trail follows long sections of wall with some of the most impressive sections being along this stretch. When the wall was constructed it was up to six metres high and three metres wide, which is evident when you see the scale of the ruins remaining today.

WALLTOWN & THE WHIN SILL

DISTANCE: 17.7KM/11MILES » **TOTAL ASCENT:** 322M/1,056FT » **START GR:** NY 668658 » **TIME:** ALLOW 6 HOURS **SATNAV:** CA8 7HF » **MAP:** OS EXPLORER OL43, HADRIAN'S WALL, 1:25,000 » **REFRESHMENTS:** WALLTOWN VISITOR CENTRE; THE GREENHEAD HOTEL, GREENHEAD » **NAVIGATION:** SOME CARE NEEDED ACROSS THIRLWALL COMMON BUT THE ROUTE IS MOSTLY WELL SIGNED.

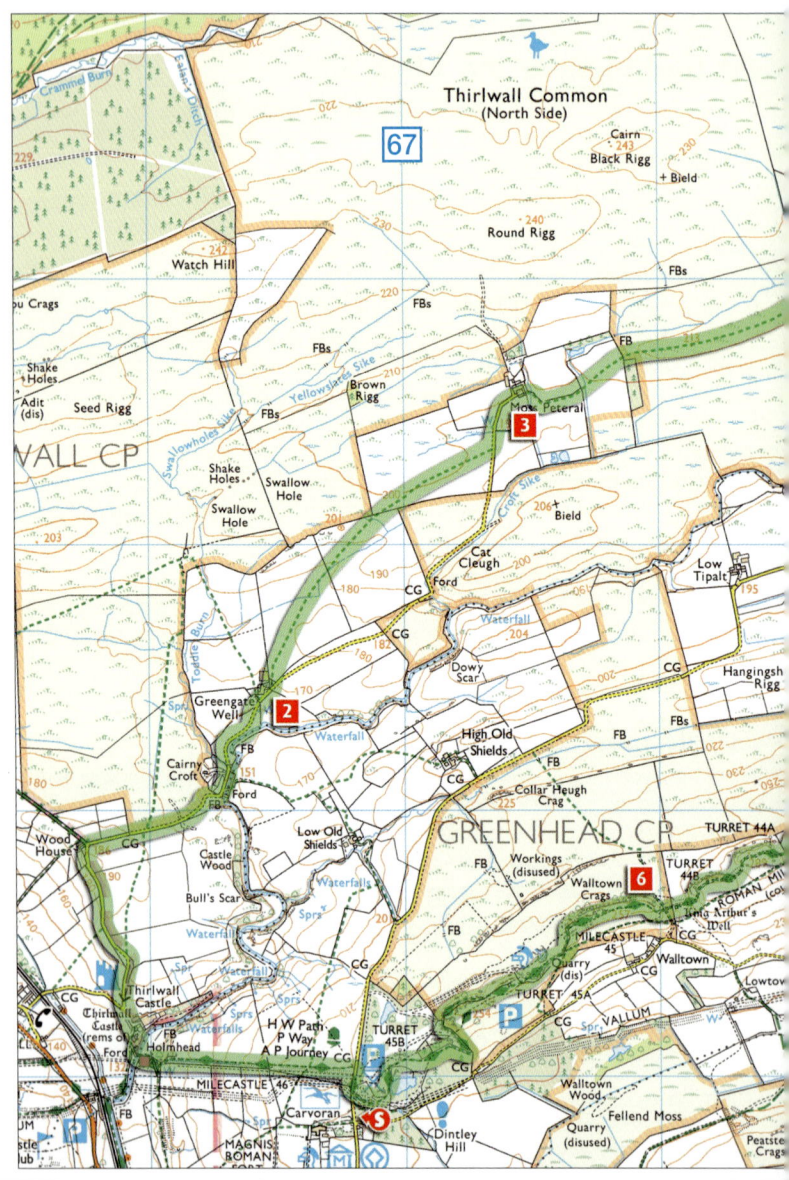

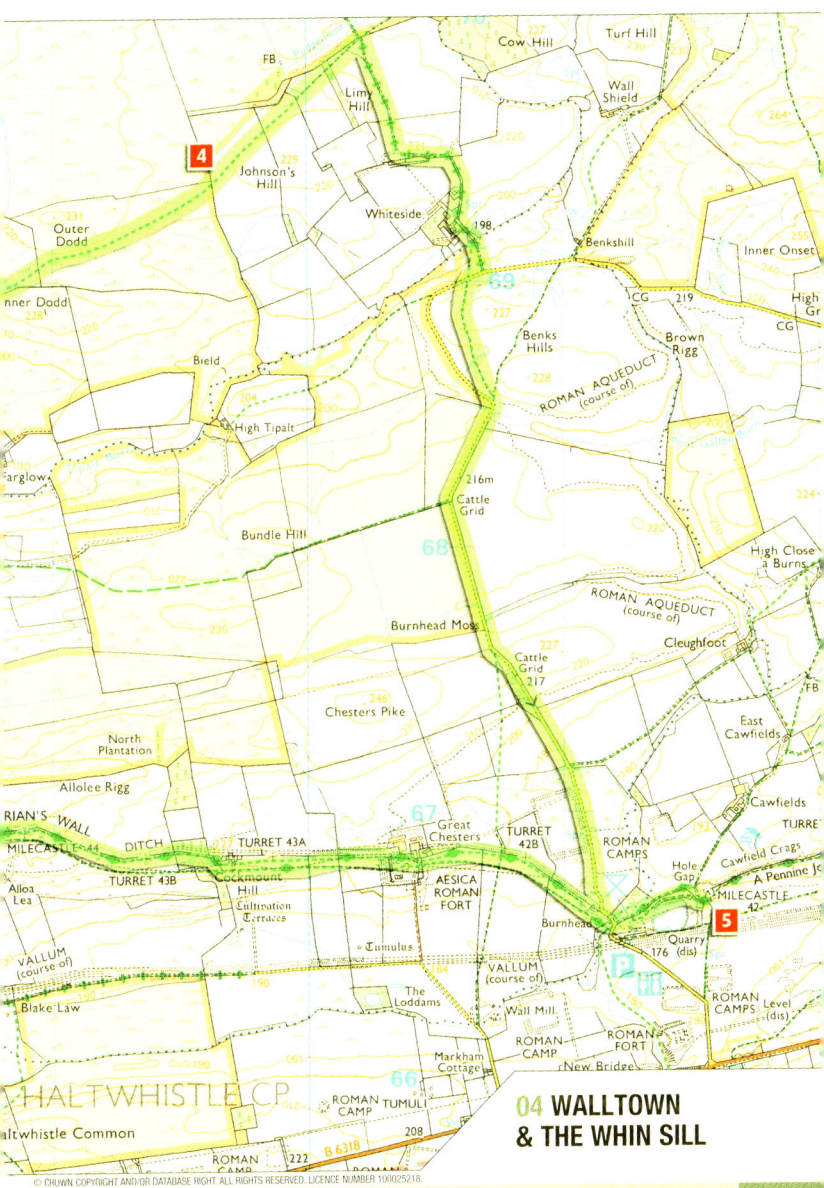

04 **WALLTOWN & THE WHIN SILL**

Directions – Walltown & the Whin Sill

1 Leave the car park via the main entrance and **turn right**. Following Hadrian's Wall Path, **turn left at a signpost for** *Thirlwall Castle* ¾. The trail briefly follows a section of Vallum (defensive ditch) on your left. Pass over a stile and head downhill to meet a track which bears left. Go through a gate; the track zigzags down to a bridge and ford. **Cross the bridge** and go up the track **straight ahead in front of castle** (leaving Hadrian's Wall Path). Walk through a farm and stay on the road uphill. Begin to get views of north face of Hadrian's Wall and Walltown Crags. **At Wood House Farm turn right**, cross a cattle grid and continue downhill following the road to Greengate Well Farm.

2 At the farm go past the first fingerpost and ahead you will see a second fingerpost. **Before the second fingerpost, at a metal gate, turn left** and go through a gate at the rear of the yard. From here head in a **diagonal-right direction** towards a small crag in the distance. Look out for a fence and a small gated wooden bridge to cross. **Stay next to the fence on the right** and go over a step in the wall. Continue towards the right-hand side of crags to a point where two fields meet at a wall. Enter the **right-hand field** over a stile. Cross the field diagonally to meet the road then **turn left** and walk along the road until you reach a farm.

3 From the farm follow the fingerpost on your **right** for *Cadgerford* 3½. Go through a gate and **around the side of the farm** to a wooden gate. Go through that gate and then follow a wall, on your left, all the way to another gate which leads to a **track heading to the north-west corner of woodland**. Beyond the trees follow a **quad track which leads off in a left-hand diagonal direction** across a field. Walk towards the fence line sitting behind small gully/burn ahead and look for a gate and a small derelict shed beyond. **Go through the gate;** at the shed note the small hill ahead and mast beyond – this is direction of travel (the ground at times has no obvious path). **Track the fence to the right for around 200m** through gates to enter large grass/marsh area. **Continue heading in the direction of the mast to a far left corner of a field and stile.**

4 Go over the stile and to the left of a hill; continue forward **to the left-hand side of trees ahead**. Pass over stiles to get to the corner of woodland and pass through trees to **cross the field beyond and meet a farm track. Turn right on the farm track** and follow to the main road beyond Whiteside Farm. At the road **turn right and after 50m turn left** on a path which goes over a small hill and **rejoins the road**. (On top of the hill you get views of a small valley which once contained a Roman aqueduct.) **Follow the road for 2.1km**, enjoying some of the best views of the north side of Hadrian's Wall. Cross a bridge then, at a junction, **turn left into Cawfields Quarry**. Beyond the car park follow the track to the rear of the lake and visit Milecastle 42 and a viewpoint over the water.

5 Retrace your steps to the junction next to the bridge. **Turn right and cross the river. Go over the wall stile on your left** (following signs for *National Trail Walltown Quarry 3¼*); enter the field and follow the track across the field with a wall on your right. Pass through a further two fields to reach Great Chesters Farm and Aesica Roman Fort. **Cross a stile and continue straight ahead to the right-hand side of Aesica Roman Fort**. Beyond the fort is a stile to enter a field; follow the track, over stiles, to reach a house. Cross the stile beyond the house to enter woodland and **follow the right-hand trail through trees**. Exit the woodland and continue to follow the wall on your right as the trail begins to climb with views behind along Hadrian's Wall and Whin Sill escarpment. Continue on the trail up to higher ground. Eventually drop down to your left and go over a stile at a wall. The trail then climbs to the top of crags, and passes another dip in the landscape, before reaching a crag overlooking a farm while passing Turret 44B. Follow steps down to a dry stone wall, cross a stile and **take the trail which hairpins right to the crag top**.

6 Follow the crags, keeping right, and you will walk alongside one of the most impressive sections of wall. As Hadrian's Wall bears left you get first view of Walltown Quarry before reaching a gated entrance on your right. Take the path into the quarry site and **follow a path on right-hand side of a bench**. After a small descent follow the **left-hand track to the car park**; or explore the many pathways of the area.

VIEW ALONG HADRIAN'S WALL

05 Classic Hadrian's Wall Country

12.7km/7.9miles

Walk in the footsteps of the Romans on this iconic circular route, following both Hadrian's Wall and the old Roman road, Stanegate. This is a true walk back in time.

The Sill » Stanegate » Vindolanda Roman Fort » Stanegate » Housesteads Roman Fort » Milecastle 37 » Sycamore Gap » The Sill

Start

The Sill: National Landscape Discovery Centre, Bardon Mill (parking charge). GR: NY 753669.

The Walk

This walk visits a popular section of Hadrian's Wall and features one of the country's most photographed trees at Sycamore Gap. In contrast to the well-walked sections along Hadrian's Wall, the route goes along one of the most important Roman roads in Britain, Stanegate – a quieter place to explore.

You begin your walk at The Sill: National Landscape Discovery Centre, built by Northumberland National Park as a gateway to the great outdoors. Take the time to explore the centre and find out about the local landscape and heritage, or visit afterwards for a bite to eat.

Leaving the centre you will soon join Stanegate – look out for the milestone as you join the road. This road ran across the country and linked forts in Carlisle and Corbridge. Constructed 50 years before the Wall, it was a marching road with forts at one-day marching intervals (13 miles). One of these forts was Vindolanda, and is the first this walk visits. Leaving Stanegate you cross the Military Road – a road named for its military function during the eighteenth-century Jacobite rising. This road is also the main culprit as to why so much stone has now disappeared from the wall.

The next fort visited is Housesteads, one of the most complete forts in Britain. Forts such as this were constructed after the wall had been started, when it was recognised that there was a need for more defence. Now on the Hadrian's Wall Path, the walk heads west passing milecastle gateways as well as smaller turret installations. The route passes the internationally known Sycamore Gap, famed by the 1991 Kevin Costner film *Robin Hood: Prince of Thieves*. The final viewpoint before returning to The Sill is Peel Crags, where to the west you can see Winshield Crags, the highest point of Hadrian's Wall.

CLASSIC HADRIAN'S WALL COUNTRY

DISTANCE: 12.7KM/7.9MILES » **TOTAL ASCENT:** 316M/1,037FT » **START GR:** NY 753669 » **TIME:** ALLOW 4.5 HOURS **SATNAV:** NE47 7AN » **MAP:** OS EXPLORER OL43, HADRIAN'S WALL, 1:25,000 » **REFRESHMENTS:** THE SILL OR TWICE BREWED INN, BARDON MILL » **NAVIGATION:** STRAIGHTFORWARD ALONG WAYMARKED TRAILS.

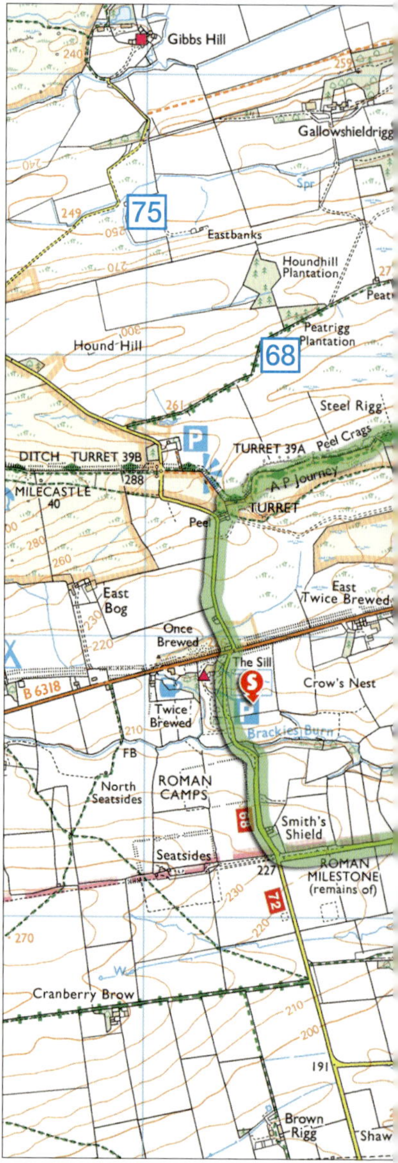

DAY WALKS IN NORTHUMBERLAND

05 CLASSIC HADRIAN'S WALL COUNTRY

Directions – Classic Hadrian's Wall Country

1 From The Sill car park join the road and **turn right**. Follow the road past Smith's Shield House to a junction; **turn left** along Stanegate. Follow the road past a thatched house towards Vindolanda Roman Fort.

2 Before the fort, **turn right** following the sign for *Henshaw 1¼, Bardon Mill 2*. Go through a gate and follow the track to the next gate with a view of Vindolanda on your left. Go through the gate and follow the cobbled track down to road; **turn left** on the road towards High Fogrigg House. As you approach the house, **turn right on a permissive path** over a stile and taking the **right-hand track**. At bottom of the track **turn left** to a gate. Go through the gate and walk to a stile on the other side of the field. Go over the stile, cross to the opposite fence line then **turn right to a further stile**. Cross into the next field and **follow the fence line on your right** all the way down to Low Fogrigg House.

3 **Turn left at the house** on to a track. Pass through two gates and continue to meet a wooden boardwalk. This leads to the bottom of the Vindolanda Roman Fort site and a bridge over a river. **Follow the signed path up to the right-hand side of the site** on to a road which leads offsite to the main road. At this point **drop left downhill** to visit the Roman Milestone (one Roman mile from the previous stone on Stanegate). **Retrace your steps back up to the road** and walk past the entrance and uphill to a T-junction. **Turn left and walk along the road.** Stay on the main road at the next junction, following *Newbrough 6*. This is the route of Stanegate. As you get to the top of the hill, with views of Grindon Lough ahead, arrive at a junction.

4 **Turn left along a bridleway** signed for *Military Road*. Pass a farm and go through **two wooden gates to your right** on to a bridleway crossing a field – marked with ground posts. The track goes uphill with views of the Military Road and a stile ahead. **Cross the stile then turn right and cross the road** – take care as this is a fast road. **Join the road on your left** going through a gate signed for *Housesteads ½*. Walk until you reach Housesteads Roman Fort.

5 **Walk between the visitor centre and the Roman Fort** to reach a gate and join the Hadrian's Wall Path National Trail. **Turn left** to walk the only section of Hadrian's Wall where you can go on top of the wall. From here follow the wall and pass Milecastle 37 before reaching the point where the Pennine Way meets Hadrian's Wall. Climb again going along Hotbank Crags with views across to Highshield Crags above Crag Lough. Drop down past Hotbank and briefly join the paved section of path. This leads **through two gates,** following the sign for *Steel Rigg 1½*.

6 Climb up through a small copse of trees, over crags and reach Sycamore Gap and its famous tree. Beyond here climb again, drop down to Milecastle 39 and then along the wall to reach the top of steep steps down to a prominent section of wall and the remains of a turret. The Sill can be seen off to your left. Follow the path along the wall (on your left) and **take a gate on your left** and walk past Peel Cottage. **Turn left** and walk along the road, crossing the Military Road (B6318) to return to The Sill.

SYCAMORE GAP

CRAGS OVERLOOKING THE COQUET VALLEY

06 Rothbury & Simonside Ridge   12.9km/8miles

One of Northumberland National Park's must-do walks. Starting out from the market town of Rothbury, this circular route takes you to a rare site dating back 4,000 years and on to one of the region's most enjoyable ridge walks.

Rothbury » Whitton » St Oswald's Way » Sharpe's Folly » Lordenshaws » Dove Crag » Simonside » Tosson Tower » River Coquet » Rothbury

Start
Cowhaugh car park, Whitton Bank Road, Rothbury. GR: NU 057015.

The Walk

The Simonside Hills form one of the most recognisable ridges in Northumberland and are visible from well beyond the boundaries of the county. Sitting on the eastern edge of Northumberland National Park, they are home to some unique aspects of Northumberland history and heritage, as well as expansive heather moorland and sandstone crags.

The walk starts on the edge of the popular market town of Rothbury, alongside the River Coquet. Rothbury has been a market town since the thirteenth century and now benefits from a quality range of shops, pubs and cafes, leading to it being a popular visitor destination.

Leaving the riverside on St Oswald's Way the trail heads towards Lordenshaws, which sits at the bottom of the main Simonside range. This walk goes past Sharpe's Folly, a tower built in the eighteenth century, through ancient deer parks and on to the Bronze Age site of Lordenshaws. Here visitors can witness the remains of hillforts and rock art, unique to only a few areas of Britain.

From Lordenshaws the walk traverses the Simonside Ridge on a mixed trail of paved sections, well-walked paths and simple boulder climbs. The ridge is very exposed in places with amazing views over Coquetdale and across to the Cheviot Hills in the north. To the south the land flattens towards the urban areas of Northumberland and out to Newcastle.

Leaving the ridge, there is a brief woodland walk to enjoy which leads down to the tiny village of Great Tosson and its fifteenth-century tower. Heading east from Great Tosson, minor roads lead down to the River Coquet before joining a riverside path back into Rothbury.

ROTHBURY & SIMONSIDE RIDGE

DISTANCE: 12.9KM/8MILES » **TOTAL ASCENT:** 413M/1,355FT » **START GR:** NU 057015 » **TIME:** ALLOW 4.5 HOURS **SATNAV:** NE65 7QR » **MAP:** OS EXPLORER OL42, KIELDER WATER & FOREST, 1:25,000 » **REFRESHMENTS:** NEWCASTLE HOUSE, ROTHBURY » **NAVIGATION:** STRAIGHTFORWARD AND WELL SIGNED.

CAIRN ON TOP OF SIMONSIDE

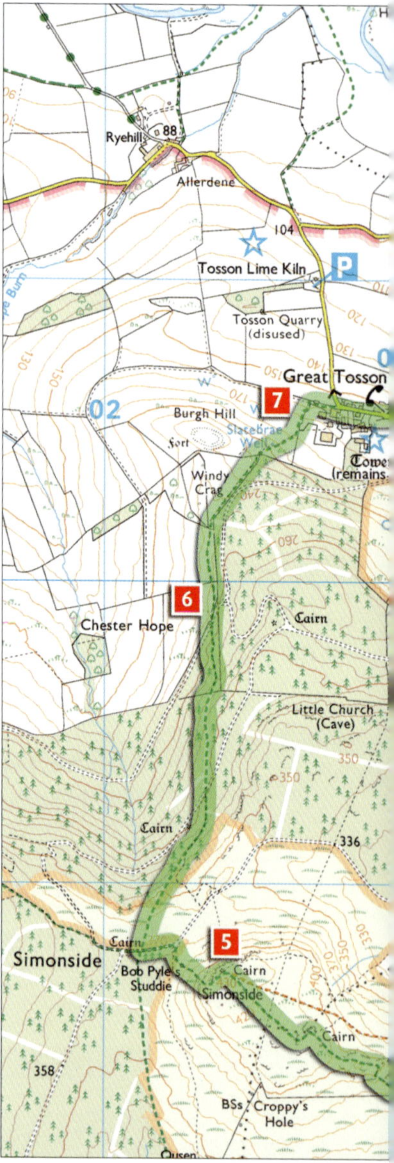

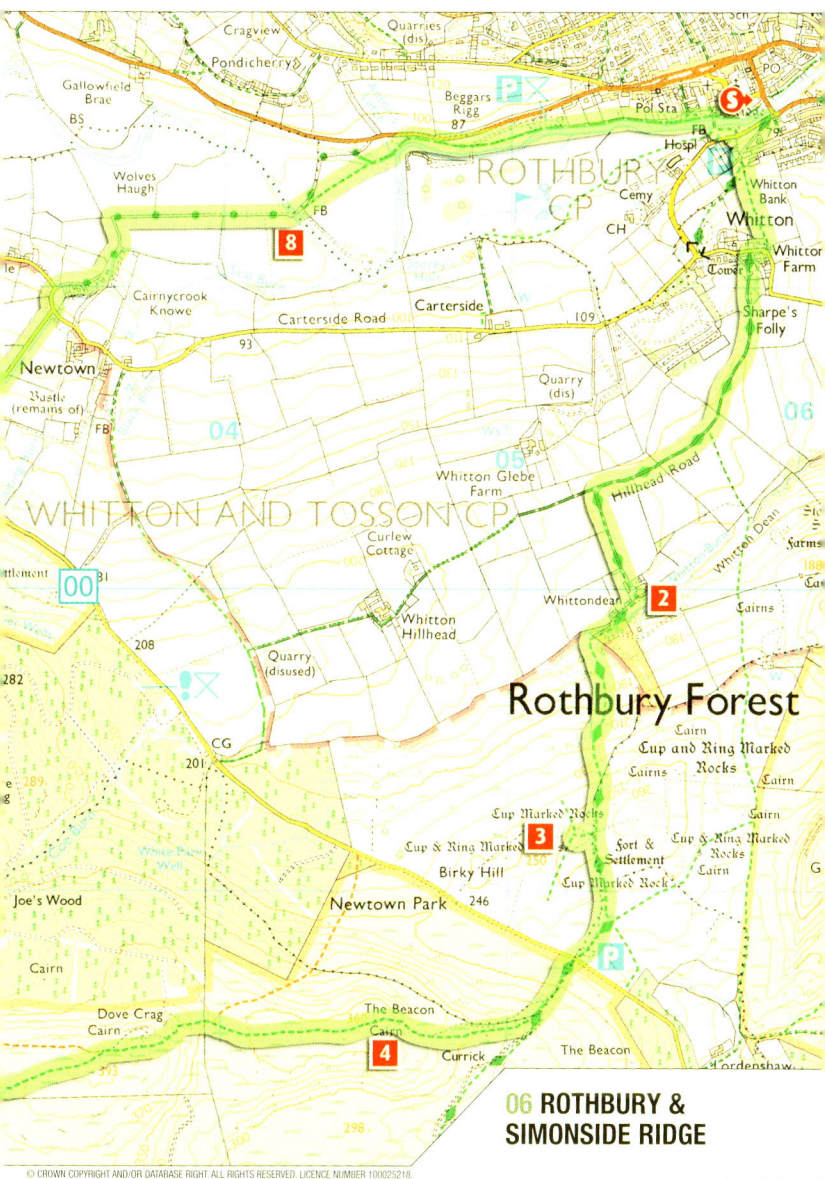

06 ROTHBURY & SIMONSIDE RIDGE

Directions – Rothbury & Simonside Ridge

- From the car park **turn left** to head towards the road bridge. At the bridge **turn right** – signed *St Oswald's Way* – and climb a steep bank. Pass some houses then **go left through a metal gate** and follow a footpath sign for *Whitton ¼*. At the **top of the hill head for the farmhouse** and take the kissing gate between buildings. At the road **turn right** and after 50m **turn left** on to a bridleway signed *Whitton Hillhead 1¼*. The track goes past Sharpe's Folly and bears right. Follow the track to the point where it begins to climb then **turn left**. Walk until you reach Whittondean Farm.

2 At Whittondean Farm **pass through two gates** between buildings and then **turn right**. The track leads downhill, across Whitton Burn, and then **off to the right through a metal gate**. At this point **bear left** and begin an uphill climb crossing the remains of a dry stone wall. Enjoy views of the Cheviot Hills behind you. After the wall **turn right** – signed *Public Footpath* and *St Oswald's Way* – and walk for 200m to a post showing three route options. **Turn right** and head towards a large rock in the distance. This is Lordenshaws Main Rock and site of Bronze Age cup and ring markings.

3 From Lordenshaws Main Rock return to the main path and go **downhill, heading south towards the car park**. Walk through the car park and leave at the main exit, then cross the road to a paved pathway up the hillside. After **200m bear right** to leave St Oswald's Way (which goes straight ahead). Follow the path to a stepped climb up to The Beacon.

4 From The Beacon **follow the visible trail**, often sandy, to a gate and steps leading to Dove Crag. The path leads between crags and a cairn to a paved route. **Keep left** on the trail to reach Old Stell Crag and follow a route amongst boulders to the top and further steps to the cairn. At the cairn the **path turns to the left** and heads along the top of boulders which sit on your right-hand side, and then the **path turns to the right** and along a lower face of boulders. Approximately 300m ahead is the cairn marking Simonside.

5 Leaving Simonside, the **path turns to the left and down a steep, stepped descent** to a forestry track. Upon meeting track **turn left.** After 100m follow a sign (on your left) to **turn right** down a track towards forest, through a heather gulley and passing footpath posts. After around 600m your route meets a forest track; **turn right** on to the track and then almost immediately **turn left into trees**. The woodland trail eventually drops down to meet another forestry track; **turn right and after 20m turn left** and through a gate to see open views over Coquetdale.

6 Go through a gate, **turn right** and the path heads along the left-hand side of forest. Pass over two stiles (wall and fence) and follow a wall heading downhill. At a sign for a *Permissive Path* on the left **turn right** and go downhill towards Great Tosson. Through gorse bushes the steep trail heads to the left-hand side of buildings to a kissing gate and stile and on to a farm road.

7 **Turn right** and walk through the farm, then continue straight ahead on to a road. Before the next road junction, on the right is Tosson Tower. After visiting the tower take the **left-hand fork** in the road and head downhill towards Newtown. **Turn left** at a junction and follow the road as it bends round to the right, eventually dropping downhill and passing Weavers Cottage. Stay on the road as it becomes a track while it bears right and follows the line of River Coquet on your left. Arrive at a footbridge.

8 **Cross the river footbridge** and immediately **turn right through a gate**, and follow the sign for *Rothbury 1 mile*. Continue across the field to a bridge, leading to a small climb on to the riverside path. **Turn right** and follow the path all the way into Rothbury. Upon reaching Rothbury take the **footbridge on your right** back to the car park.

HEATHER TRAIL

LOOKING EAST TOWARDS CUNYAN CRAGS

07 Hedgehope Hill & Breamish Valley 20.9km/13miles

Visiting the third highest peak in Northumberland, this walk explores one of the finest valleys and rivers in the Northumberland National Park.

Ingram Bridge car park » Reaveley Hill » Cunyan Crags » Dunmoor Hill » Hedgehope Hill » Linhope Spout » River Breamish » Ingram Bridge car park

Start
Ingram Bridge car park, Ingram.
GR: NU 017163.

The Walk
Passing through the small village of Ingram, the River Breamish and its valley make up one of the most picturesque locations in Northumberland National Park.

The Breamish Valley was once a tree-filled landscape and has transformed over millennia as populations grew and hardy rural communities developed. From the farming settlements along the valley floor, to the Iron Age forts on the hilltops, this land bears the scars of man's time in Northumberland.

A short walk from Ingram is Reaveleyhill Cottage, a fascinating reminder of the local farming heritage as the former home of a shepherd and his family. The view from Reaveley Hill looks across to the various hillforts on the south side of the valley. Brough Law, the most prominent of the hills, was the site of a large Iron Age fort with numerous stone ramparts to give it a considerable defensive position.

Beyond Reaveley Hill is Cunyan Crags, the boulder gateway to Dunmoor Hill with amazing views across to Kidland Forest and the Border Ridge (see route 11). At 569 metres, Dunmoor Hill is towered over by one of Northumberland National Park's most recognisable peaks, Hedgehope Hill (714 metres). The summit of Hedgehope Hill enjoys 360-degree views with The Cheviot (see route 10) sitting to the north, and unbroken views of the coast to the east.

The slopes of Hedgehope Hill and the various burns that flow down it, lead to Linhope Burn and Linhope Spout – one of the region's most spectacular waterfalls at eighteen metres high and falling into a five-metre pool. Linhope Burn then leads back through the hamlet of Linhope and to the floor of the valley, a fitting companion along the gorse-lined walk along to Ingram.

HEDGEHOPE HILL & BREAMISH VALLEY

DISTANCE: 20.9KM/13MILES » **TOTAL ASCENT:** 777M/2,549FT » **START GR:** NU 017163 » **TIME:** ALLOW 7 HOURS **SATNAV:** NE66 4LT » **MAP:** OS EXPLORER OL16, THE CHEVIOT HILLS, 1:25,000 » **REFRESHMENTS:** INGRAM CAFE, INGRAM » **NAVIGATION:** A WELL-WALKED TRAIL WITH SOME SIGNS; CARE NEEDED WHEN VISIBILITY IS POOR.

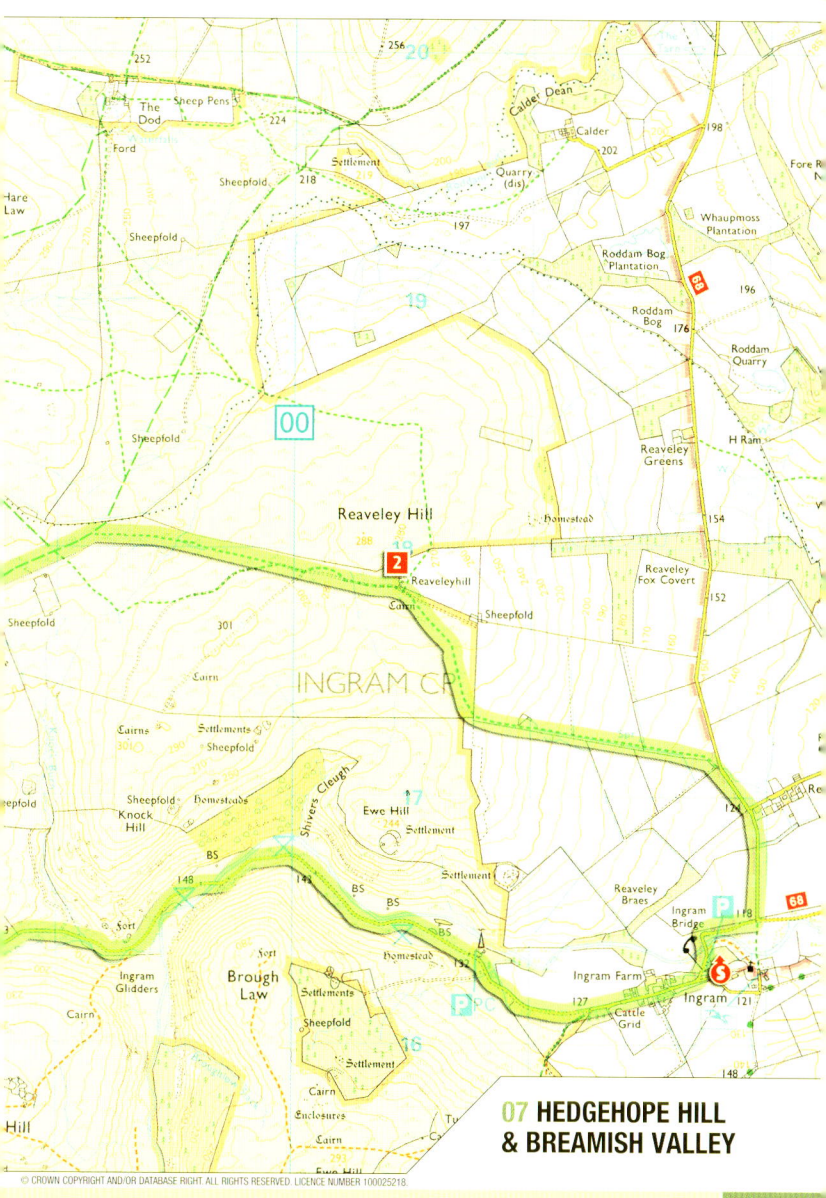

07 **HEDGEHOPE HILL & BREAMISH VALLEY**

Directions – Hedgehope Hill & Breamish Valley

1. From the small car park **turn right** and head over the bridge (the path on the right before the bridge leads to Ingram Cafe). Follow the road then **turn left** towards Reaveley Farm. Once past the farm **turn left** at the signpost marked *Reaveleyhill 1*. Follow the right-hand track up the hill – with a fence on your left – all the way up and through a gate. Beyond the gate the track goes through a dry stone wall and another gate. Reaveleyhill Cottage can be seen off to your right-hand side. **After 50m take the worn grass track on your right** leading to the cottage, passing through a gate/stile on route.

2. Leave the cottage to the left (when facing) and **follow the (quad) track** ahead sitting alongside the fence. Some sections may be boggy and heading in towards the fence can ease passing. Remain near the fence for roughly 1km and when a sheepfold appears to your left and you arrive at a junction, **turn left** to head towards it on the track. Staying on northern side of the sheepfold the track leads to a gate/stile marked *Public Bridleway*. Going forward you reach a **three-way signpost; turn right** on a footpath to a gate. Go through the gate; the path leads to another gate but before it take the **track bearing left uphill**, with a fence on your right. The track goes up and through the middle of Cunyan Crags. From the crags enjoy views of the Breamish Valley and across to Brough Law hillfort.

3. From the crags continue to follow the fence line, through a gate, and up on to Dunmoor Hill. Descend Dunmoor Hill by staying on the same track (with the fence on your right) heading downhill and curving to the left past forestry works on the right. **At a junction of fences continue straight ahead through a gate** and go up to Hedgehope Hill and its trig point at 714m. As you head up **look out for quad track on the left** (approximately 50m from the gate) – this is the return route after visiting the summit.

4. Leave Hedgehope Hill by **retracing your steps down same track** then **turn right along the quad track,** which sits alongside a burn and heads downhill. Stay on the track, pass over a cattle grid and, **at a signpost for** *Hedgehope 2½*, **turn left** and go along a track and over a bridge. After 100m on this track, and beyond small line of bushes/trees, **turn left and follow the line of the river** on your left. The track drops steeply down to the river to reach Linhope Spout.

5 From the waterfall follow the line of the river away from the falls. Reach a fence and **turn right** on to a steep track to the top. **Turn left and go through a gate** – signed *Hartside Farm 1, Linhope ¼*. Follow the tree line on your left all the way down into Linhope, then walk through houses and out on to the main road. **Follow the road as it leads uphill to Hartside Farm.**

6 **Continue straight ahead** along the road. When the road drops to the valley floor and runs alongside the river, you can see Brough Law hillfort straight ahead. Shortly afterwards the road crosses the River Breamish; you can choose to walk on the road or by the river to return to the car park.

REAVELEY HILL

YEAVERING BELL

08 Ad Gefrin

18.8km/11.7miles

A memorable walk on the northern edge of the Cheviot Hills, visiting ancient settlements in search of the elusive Cheviot Goat.

Wooler » St Cuthbert's Way » Wooler Common » Yeavering Bell » White Law » Humbleton Hill » Wooler

Start

The Cheviot Centre, adjacent to Padgepool Place car park, Wooler. GR: NT 989281.

The Walk

Wooler is a traditional farming town, and its position at the north of Northumberland National Park gives rise to it being known as the 'Gateway to the Cheviots'. Its range of amenities makes it a popular place for walkers, including those trekking St Cuthbert's Way on the final leg to Holy Island.

Following St Cuthbert's Way out of the town, the landscape quickly changes to vast heather moorlands stretching out to The Cheviot in the south-west. The moors are at their best in August when the heather blooms and becomes a sea of purple, while also being home to a range of game birds such as grouse and pheasants.

The nature seeker will regularly come across bird life in this rich natural habitat, but it is only the patient and hardy walkers who will meet the elusive Cheviot Goat. These feral animals are believed to have arrived during Neolithic times as domestic stock, to later become feral when sheep became favoured. This walk, and the hill it visits, is named after these goats.

Yeavering Bell, sitting south of Old Yeavering, was previously referred to as 'Gefrin' meaning 'hill of the goats'. The bell (hill) has twin peaks and is encircled by stone which once made up one of the largest hillforts in the north of England. The names of Yeavering and Gefrin are intertwined through the ages with the site now referred to as Ad Gefrin, 'near the hill of the goats'. Sitting at the foot of the hill is the seventh-century site which was home to the palace of King Edwin of Northumbria.

Yeavering Bell is one of many hillforts in the area. With their characteristic conical shape, these hills were formed by glacial meltwater creating steep slopes to make ideal defensive bases. Another classic example of these land formations is Humbleton Hill, which stands guard over Wooler, marking the end of the walk.

AD GEFRIN

DISTANCE: 18.8KM/11.7MILES » **TOTAL ASCENT:** 685M/2,247FT » **START GR:** NT 989281 » **TIME:** ALLOW 6.5 HOURS
SATNAV: NE71 6BL » **MAP:** OS EXPLORER OL16, THE CHEVIOT HILLS, 1:25,000 » **REFRESHMENTS:** DODDINGTON DAIRY MILK BAR, WOOLER » **NAVIGATION:** STRAIGHTFORWARD ON CLEAR PATHS AND WAYMARKED TRAILS.

Directions – Ad Gefrin

From The Cheviot Centre walk along Padgepool Place then **turn right** to walk into town. Pass the bus station on your left then **turn right** on to Ramsey's Lane. Walk up the road for 500m until you reach a signpost on the left. **Turn left here through a gate** (following the sign for *St Cuthbert's Way*); follow the path uphill. At the trees go **through a gate and straight ahead**. At a fence line **turn left, and immediately right,** to rejoin St Cuthbert's Way and continue ahead keeping to the left-hand side as you leave a clearing. Leave trees via a gate and **turn right along a track**; meet a further track and **turn right towards a house**. At a burn go through a metal gate on to a road.

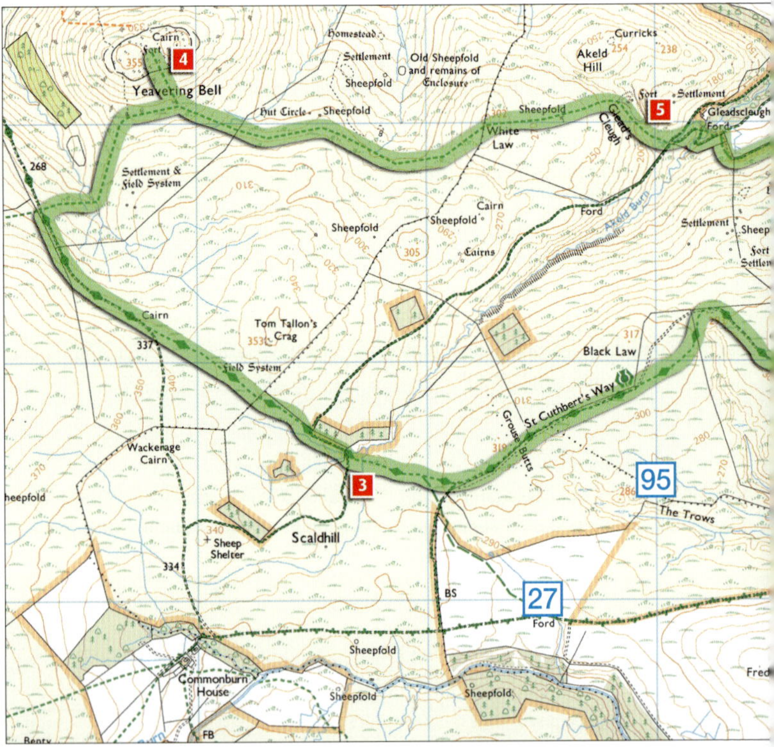

2 Turn right and walk along the road to a car park. Walk through the car park to join the left-hand track going up into trees signed *St Cuthbert's Way*. After a small climb through trees go through a gate and **bear left** on a track. Go through a gate to a signpost and **turn left** (following signs for *St Cuthbert's Way*) through another gate. **Turn immediately right** and follow the fence on your right. Enjoy views of The Cheviot to left. Stay on St Cuthbert's Way through a gate and continue on the trail through heather moorland to **reach a gate on your right-hand side**. Go through the gate and continue ahead with the wall now on your left-hand side. The track then **bears right to a gate and small copse of trees**.

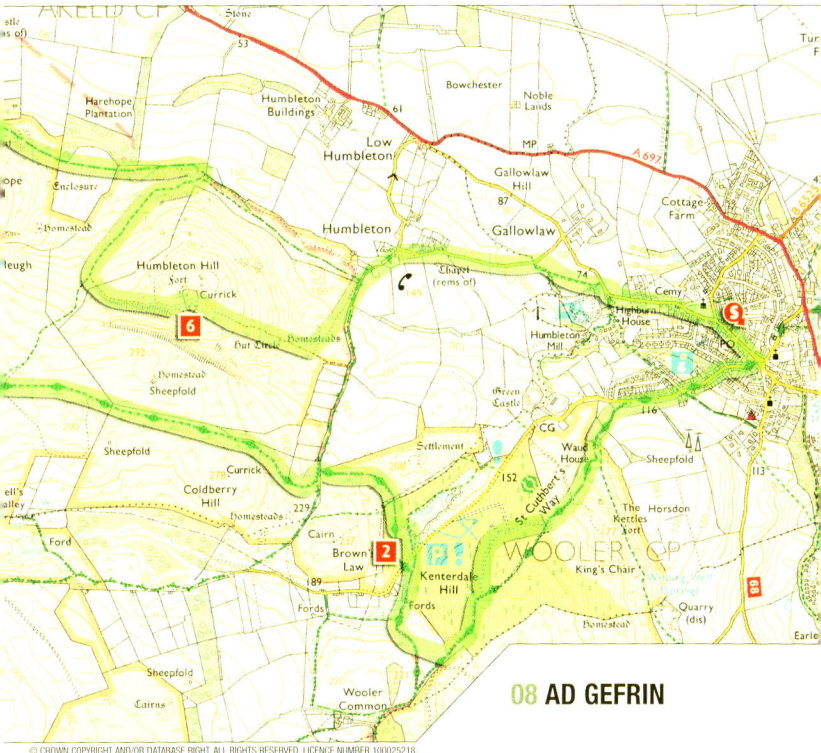

08 **AD GEFRIN**

Directions – Ad Gefrin

3 Beyond the trees look for a stile over a wall; cross the stile and follow the track. Yeavering Bell is on your right. The track reaches a multi-directional sign (on the ground); **turn right** for *Yeavering Bell ½*. Climb towards the top of the hill; close to a ridge of stone notice a track going off to your right and downhill – this is the exit route. Explore the Iron Age hillfort.

4 From Yeavering Bell retrace your steps to the track noted on your way up; **turn left** along the track. Follow the trail to cross a stile and follow the track leading to the top of White Law. Go over a stile and follow arrow signs **past a sheepfold and bearing right** above Glead's Cleugh.

5 Drop down to **cross a stile, turn left, then follow the right-hand track** towards a house. Before the house the track weaves up to the right and climbs to a fence on your right. **Turn right** here (signed *Public Bridleway*). Follow the wall uphill to reach gate on your left; **go through the gate** and then walk around base of Harehope Hill. After a stile drop down to further stile. Once at the **base of Humbleton Hill look out for track running to the right**. Take this route which joins a wider track all the way to top of Humbleton Hill.

6 **Continue straight ahead** to leave Humbleton Hill on the permissive path/hillfort trail which drops down to the base of the hill looking over Wooler. Notice the track heading from right to left to a corner of a field. **Turn left** to meet this track; go through a gate to meet a farm road. **Turn left and walk into Humbleton**. At a T-junction in Humbleton **turn right** and follow the road towards Wooler. After 400m look out for seat and signpost. **Turn right** here and follow the track across to the corner of the field and a gate. Go through the gate and **turn right** along the road which leads all the way back to The Cheviot Centre.

FROM HUMBLETON HILL TOWARDS WOOLER

WHITELAW NICK

09 College Valley

23.3km/14.5miles

This circular trail through the most northerly valley in Northumberland National Park encompasses both St Cuthbert's Way and the Pennine Way before returning alongside College Burn.

Hethpool » St Cuthbert's Way » Whitelaw Nick » Pennine Way » The Schil » Auchope Shelter » Hen Hole » College Burn » Hethpool

Start
Hethpool car park, Hethpool.
GR: NT 894280.

The Walk

The College Valley is a jewel in Northumberland National Park's crown given its rural charm and idyllic setting on the northern edge of the Cheviot Hills. An ancient landscape of Bronze Age hillforts and farmsteads – little has changed since the time of Admiral Lord Collingwood, who once owned and lived on the Hethpool estate.

St Cuthbert's Way crosses the top of the College Burn on its 100-kilometre route from Lindisfarne to Melrose in the Scottish Borders. Joining St Cuthbert's Way in Hethpool, the trail climbs away from the Elsdon Burn to the border fence and views into Scotland. It's here that St Cuthbert's Way meets the Pennine Way (only a few miles from its end in Kirk Yetholm) and begins its journey south along the Border Ridge.

The undulating hills of the Border Ridge make for a strenuous and rewarding trek, with the summit of The Schil (601 metres) providing a welcome stop and viewpoint. The College Valley below sits in the shadow of the The Cheviot (see route 10), and the Auchope Shelter and Hen Hole ahead.

The steady descent from The Schil opens up views of the Hen Hole, above which is the source of the College Burn, and brings into focus the Three Sisters Waterfall which carries the burn down the rocky gorge. A place of both folklore and wild beauty, here at the head of the College Valley is a fitting start for the return journey back along the road to Hethpool. The few whitewashed houses along the road are the homes of the hardy inhabitants who still live in this hidden corner of Northumberland.

COLLEGE VALLEY

DISTANCE: 23.3KM/14.5MILES » **TOTAL ASCENT:** 772M/2,533FT » **START GR:** NT 894280 » **TIME:** ALLOW 7.5 HOURS **SATNAV:** NE71 6TW » **MAP:** OS EXPLORER OL16, THE CHEVIOT HILLS, 1:25,000 » **REFRESHMENTS:** DODDINGTON DAIRY MILK BAR, WOOLER » **NAVIGATION:** STRAIGHTFORWARD.

DAY WALKS IN NORTHUMBERLAND

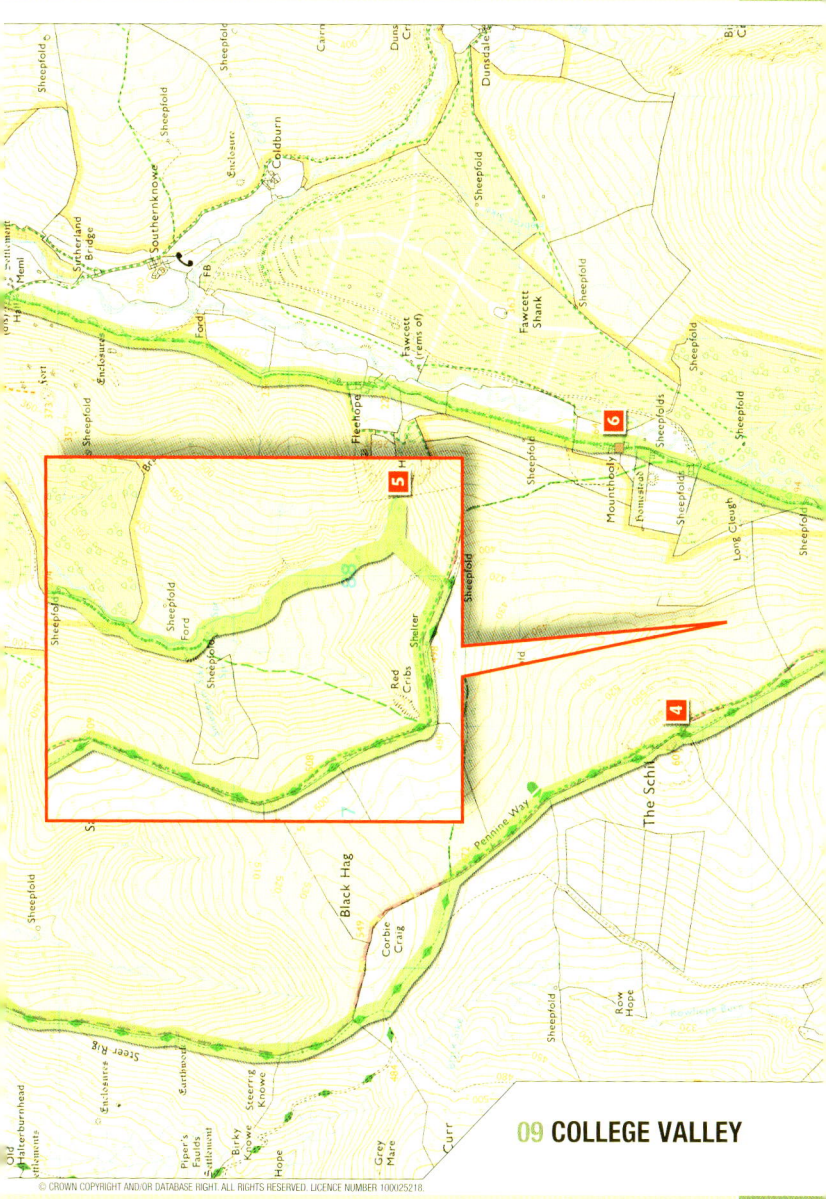

Directions – College Valley

1 **Turn right** from the car park to head towards Hethpool. Stay on the road as it curves to the left and walk to some livestock pens. **Turn left** along the track (St Cuthbert's Way). After 1.3km arrive at a track junction.

2 **Take the right-hand track** and walk towards farm buildings in the distance. At a house the track bends around to the left with a sign for *Border Ridge 1½*. Stay on the track as it climbs to the right and then through some gates. Stay on St Cuthbert's Way and go over a stile. **Stay on the right-hand trail, heading downhill,** and then climb again around the right-hand side of a hill to reach a felled forest. A temporary path leads through trees and on to a path up a hill. **At the top of the hill look for, and follow, a quad track to your left** which leads to a gate in a wall.

3 Go through the gate and **turn left** next to a signpost for *Pennine Way Windy Gyle 10½*. Drop down a bank and climb (with a wall on your left) to a stile. **Cross the stile and turn left.** Follow the trail to Steerrig Knowe and a gate marked *Pennine Way National Trail*. At the next gate (marked *Kelso Path)* and with Black Hag ahead, **bear right down a track,** with a crag to your left and a post on your right. At a signpost for *Windy Gyle 7¾*, head towards Windy Gyle following the track up to The Schil.

4 From The Schil **continue straight ahead**, downhill, and meet a gate/stile. There are some paved sections and some boggy sections on the route. Follow the fence on your right all the way downhill to reach Auchope Shelter. **Continue for 150m then take a track on the left** dropping down towards the College Burn. **Head to the burn and turn right** to face waterfalls.

5 Explore the waterfall area before retracing your steps and then **follow the line of the College Burn**, heading downstream. Follow the trail until it reaches a quad track past metal sheds and a sheepfold. Continue ahead all the way to Mounthooly Bunkhouse, following *Footpath* signs.

6 Beyond Mounthooly Bunkhouse follow the tarmac road along the valley to reach Cuddystone Hall and a war memorial. Stay on the road and follow the valley all the way back to Hethpool.

HEN HOLE AND THE THREE SISTERS WATERFALL

HARTHOPE LINN

10 The Cheviot

17.5km/10.9miles

A challenging circular to Northumberland's highest peak: The Cheviot. The walk also visits the Harthope Valley and the site of a World War II plane crash.

Langleeford » Scald Hill » The Cheviot » Braydon Crag » Cairn Hill » Harthope Linn » Langleeford

Start
Parking area north-east of Langleeford. GR: NT 954225.

The Walk
The Cheviot, standing at 815 metres, is the highest peak in Northumberland and boasts views into Scotland, along the east coast, and across to the Lake District. It is the last major peak when heading north on the Pennine Way.

This is a challenging and direct route up to the once volcanic, flat summit, now a rich, carbon-filled peat bog. The trail from Langleeford is well walked and upon reaching the top there is a paved stone walkway to the distinctive trig point.

Beyond The Cheviot is Cairn Hill from where the Pennine Way heads north on its final leg. Before reaching Cairn Hill, the route offers the chance to walk across scarred moorland to Braydon Crag, which commands amazing views over the College Valley. It is also the final resting place for the remains of a B-17G Flying Fortress which crashed on 16 December 1944, killing two of the nine men on board. The remaining crew were rescued by local shepherds and Northumberland's most famous sheepdog, Sheila. This is one of a number of World War II crash sites across the Cheviot Hills.

Leaving the exposed trails of The Cheviot in pursuit of the Harthope Burn, a lush bracken corridor weaves along a secluded and peaceful valley floor, passing one of the the many linns (waterfalls) in the national park.

Langleeford Hope brings the trail to a farm track with Hedgehope Hill (see route 7) sitting above and the leisurely walk back to Langleeford ahead.

THE CHEVIOT
DISTANCE: 17.5KM/10.9MILES » **TOTAL ASCENT:** 705M/2,313FT » **START GR:** NT 954225 » **TIME:** ALLOW 6 HOURS **SATNAV:** NE71 6RG » **MAP:** OS EXPLORER OL16, THE CHEVIOT HILLS, 1:25,000 » **REFRESHMENTS:** DODDINGTON DAIRY MILK BAR, WOOLER » **NAVIGATION:** A VARIETY OF NATURAL FEATURES COMBINE TO MAKE A STRAIGHTFORWARD TRAIL; CARE REQUIRED ON ROUTE TO/FROM BRAYDON CRAG.

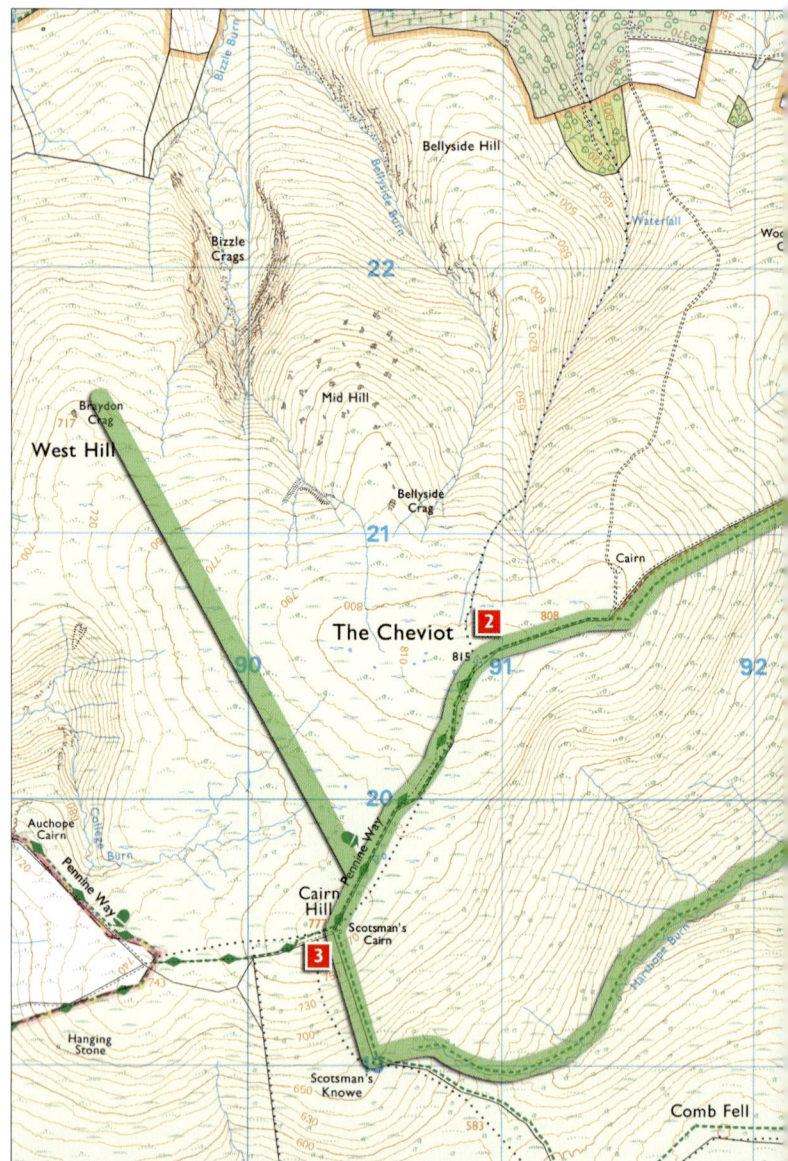

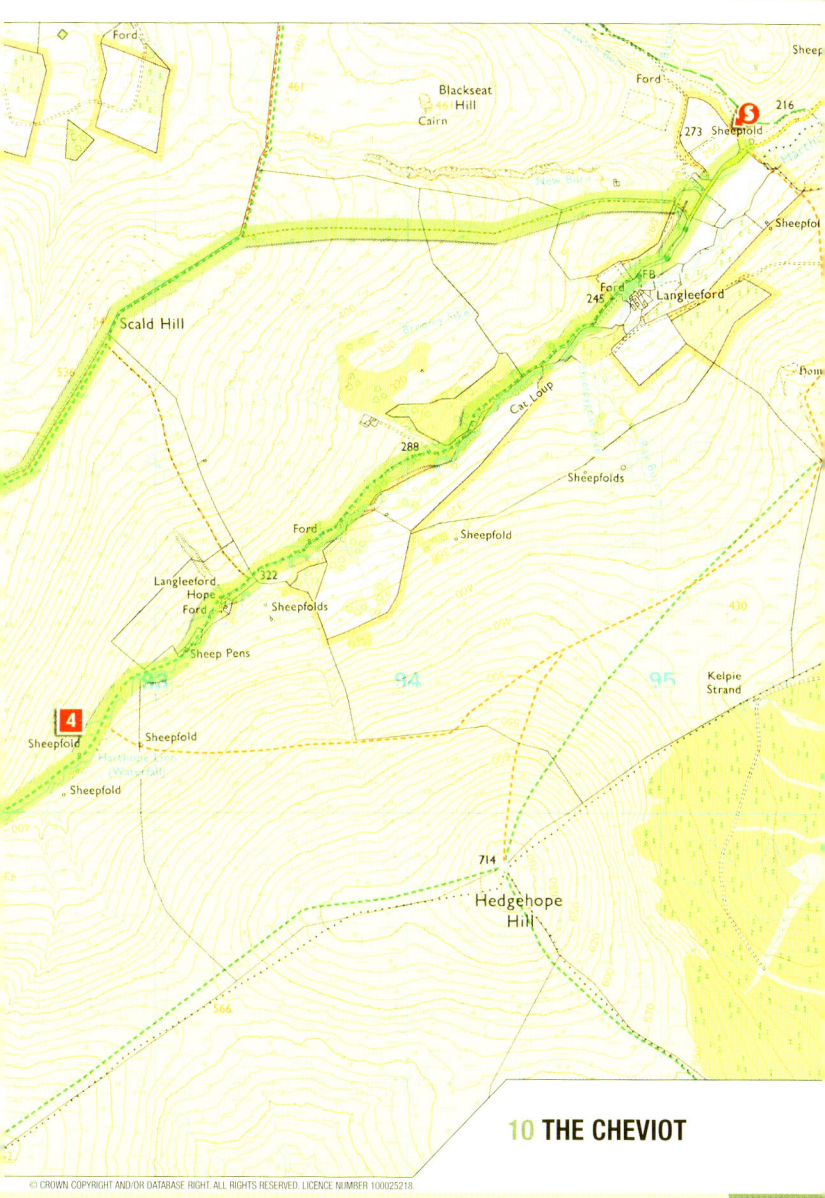

Directions – The Cheviot

1 From the parking area walk south-west along the road. Upon reaching a signpost for *Scald Hill 1½*, **turn right** and go through a gate. **Take the left-hand path**, climbing immediately, up to and over a stile. **Turn right** and continue to follow the path uphill. Upon meeting a fence cross a stile, then continue ahead uphill. Pass shooting hides and a handrail fence on your right-hand side and continue to the top of Scald Hill (going through a gate and stile), with Hedgehope Hill sitting to your left. From Scald Hill continue to follow the fence line on your right-hand side, passing two cairns and continuing uphill to meet a stile. **Cross the stile and continue on to the paved path**; follow this all the way to the trig point and summit of The Cheviot.

2 From the summit continue straight ahead (now on the Pennine Way) and **walk for around 900m** looking for a corner of a **fence that protrudes sharply out to the right**. At this point* take a **bearing of 330 degrees** and walk across moorland for around 2km. As you begin to descend you will see Braydon Crag ahead overlooking the College Valley beyond; walk towards the crag. About 150m before the crag you will begin to see the remains of a B-17G plane crash – marked out with white poles. After exploring the area **retrace your steps** back from Braydon Crag to the Pennine Way. On reaching the path **turn right** and walk to meet the fingerposts on top of Cairn Hill.

> **OR** *To miss out the walk to Braydon Crags continue straight ahead and follow the Pennine Way to the summit of Cairn Hill.

3 From the summit follow the signpost for *Langleeford 3¾*. This will take you **over the left-hand stile**, next to Scotsman's Cairn and down the hillside. **(The fence should be on your right.)** Descend to the next signpost for *Langleeford 3½*. At this point **turn left** and begin to follow the track leading to start of Harthope Burn. Follow the track along the burn to visit Harthope Linn (on your right).

4 Beyond the waterfall **stay on the track to reach Langleeford Hope** which sits in a small copse of trees. **Leave the burn by going over a stile on your left** and follow the track through trees and up past a house. Go through a gate and past a signpost on your left for *Scald Hill ¾, Cheviot 2¼*. Continue on the track past Langleeford and through a kissing gate to get back to the start.

BRIDGE OVER THE USWAY BURN

11 Barrowburn & the Border Ridge   19.6km/12.2miles

A hike up on to the Border Ridge from the Coquet Valley, enjoying views into both England and Scotland, before returning along the Usway Burn past Davidson's Linn.

Wedder Leap » Hindside Knowe » The Street » Black Braes » Windy Gyle » Davidson's Linn » Murder Cleugh » Wedder Leap

Start
Wedder Leap car park, Barrowburn.
GR: NT 866103.

The Walk
The northern edge of Northumberland National Park borders with Scotland on what is known as the Border Ridge. This classic walking route gives excellent views across both southern Scotland and Northumberland, into a remote and wild landscape.

Walking from Barrowburn in the Coquet Valley, the ascent up to the Border Ridge follows The Street – an ancient drove road where cattle would be brought from the Highlands to be sold in England. This honest trade was often accompanied by illicit activities such as whisky smuggling and gambling, with many of the perpetrators to be found in the now disappeared Slimefoot Pub just over the burn.

The summit of Windy Gyle at 619 metres gives a good indication of the weather to be found in this area, and leaving the exposed ridge is to be enjoyed as much as the sheltered peace of Davidson's Linn below. This was another popular place for eighteenth-century whisky smugglers as evidenced by the remains of a whisky still nearby.

Just before returning to Barrowburn, the dark history of this area concludes when we pass Murder Cleugh and the memorial stone to Isabella Sudden. Robert Lumsden, a dangerous local character, is said to have murdered Isabella in 1610 – if history is true she wasn't his only victim!

The walk concludes with a hasty retreat over Barrow Law, enjoying views over Barrowburn Farm and down into the Coquet Valley.

BARROWBURN & THE BORDER RIDGE

DISTANCE: 19.6KM/12.2MILES » **TOTAL ASCENT:** 623M/2,044FT » **START GR:** NT 866103 » **TIME:** ALLOW 6.5 HOURS
SATNAV: NE65 7BP » **MAP:** OS EXPLORER OL16, THE CHEVIOT HILLS, 1:25,000 » **REFRESHMENTS:** THE STAR INN, HARBOTTLE; ROSE & THISTLE, ALWINTON » **NAVIGATION:** STRAIGHTFORWARD ON TO BORDER RIDGE; SOME CARE REQUIRED ON RETURN ROUTE AFTER THE WATERFALL.

DAVIDSON'S LINN

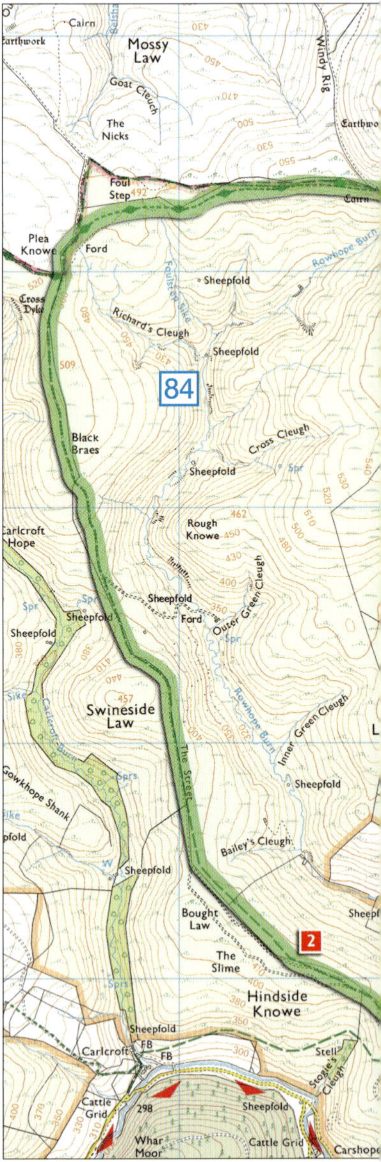

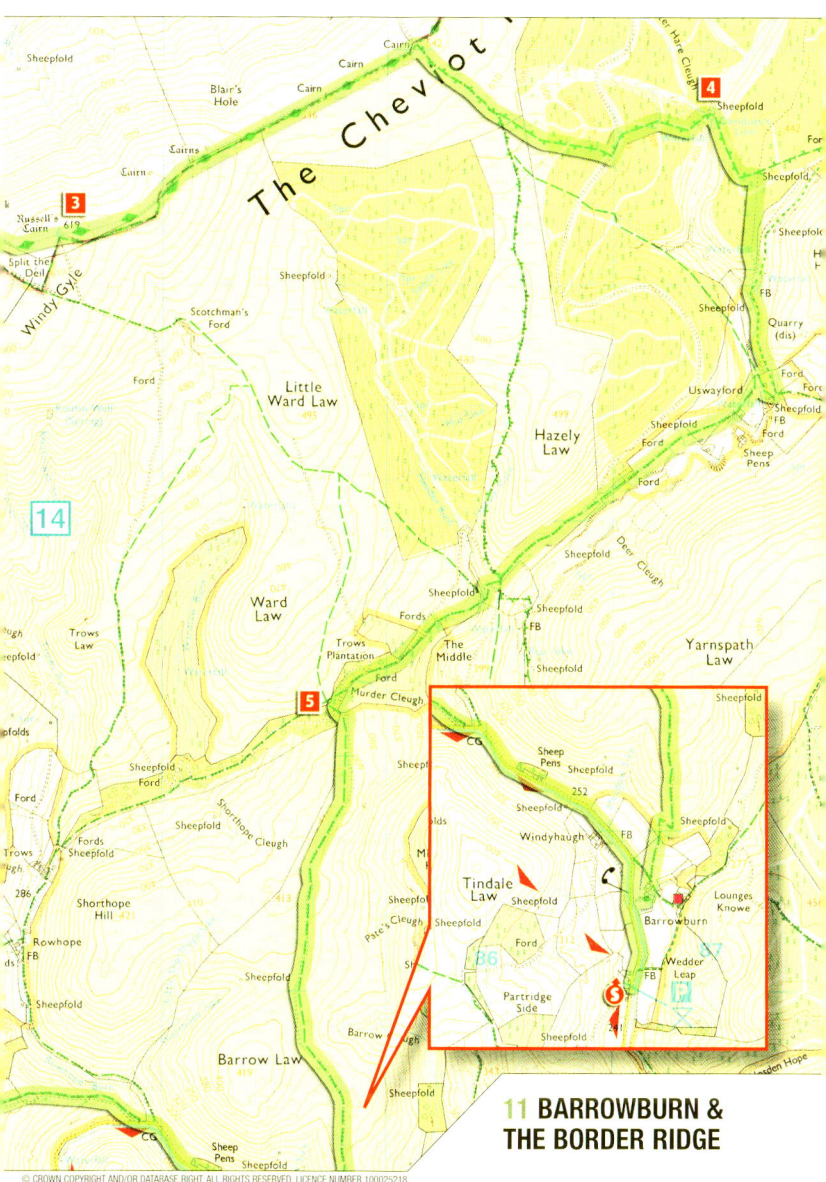

11 BARROWBURN & THE BORDER RIDGE

11 BARROWBURN & THE BORDER RIDGE – NORTHUMBERLAND NATIONAL PARK

Directions – Barrowburn & the Border Ridge

⑤ Setting out from Wedder Leap car park, **turn left** and head along the road past Barrowburn Farm on your right. Stay on the road past a small copse of trees to reach a bridge over Rowhope Burn. Approaching the bridge the onward path can be seen going up the hillside ahead. Just beyond the bridge **turn right**, following the signpost for *The Street, Border Ridge 3*, and begin to climb on the right-hand side of a fence line. After 300m go over a stile (there is a copse of trees to your right); the path then bears right and passes over a small rise on Hindside Knowe.

2 Pass over the stile ahead to the right-hand side of a fence and continue ahead on the track to gain views of the Border Ridge ahead. Reach a fingerpost marked *Pennine Way*. Stay on the track and once through a gate marked *Kelso Path*, **turn right and follow the Pennine Way** towards Windy Gyle and walking adjacent to the ridgeline. At double gates, **take the right-hand gate** and follow the fence all the way to Russell's Cairn on the summit of Windy Gyle.

3 From Windy Gyle follow the fingerpost for *Pennine Way, The Schill 7*. Various footpaths lead away from the cairn in the same direction; the footpath to the right-hand side of the fence is often easier to follow as sections are paved. Walk past a number of cairns on your left to reach a path junction. **Turn right**, leaving the Pennine Way, following the sign for *Restricted Byway for Clennel Street Alwinton 9*. Follow the track to the next signpost. **Turn left** here (following *Salters Road High Bleakhope 5*) and **walk to a stile**. Continue through the next stile into trees and walk for 200m through trees to meet a track. **Turn left** along the track; **after 50m turn right** (following *Restricted Byway*) and walk through to an opening in the trees above Usway Burn. Make your way along the track as it **curves to the left down to a sheepfold and bridge**. Just before the bridge **take the track on your right** and drop down to the side of Davidson's Linn (a waterfall).

4 Return to the bridge. **Cross the bridge** and follow the track along the left-hand side of Usway Burn. Just after the track curves to the left, **turn right** on to a muddy quad track which goes into a gap in the trees. Follow the track through trees and **drop down towards the river bearing left to a small burn** (which is easier to cross). Cross the burn on your left and follow the track above the main river **towards grey farm sheds** ahead and then **cross a bridge**. Keep following the track as it **drops down into the valley of Hepden Burn**; the track curves to the right, then to the left, before rising up to the trees ahead. Join a firm track, which briefly goes to grass track, then **turn left** around the head of the tree line to a gate. Go through the gate (on the left is a sign for Murder Cleugh).

5 From the gate the track bears to the right away from trees. **Continue following the trail** all the way to above Barrowburn Farm. **Walk down to the farm** and around the rear of the building to the access road which meets the main road. **Turn left** on the road and walk back to the car park.

VIEW OVER BLACK BRAES

SIDWOOD FOREST

12 Border Reivers & Tarset Burn   17.7km/11miles

From the bastle houses of the sixteenth century to the disused railway lines of the nineteenth century: explore Border Reiver country and the history and heritage around the Tarset Burn.

Greenhaugh » River Tyne Trail » Thorneyburn Station » Sidwood » Tarset Bastle Trail » Black Middens » Greenhaugh

Start

Small car park opposite the Holly Bush Inn, Greenhaugh. GR: NY 795873.

The Walk

Greenhaugh is a small village at the heart of Border Reiver country. The time of the Border Reivers (fifteenth and sixteenth centuries) was less about the Anglo-Scottish Wars and more about fighting for your *Grayne* (surname). Following the Tarset Burn out of Greenhaugh, it guides us down to where it joins the River North Tyne. This section of the Tyne was the route of the long-time lost Border Counties Railway, which served the many villages from Hexham up towards the Scottish Borders (see route 13). The most prominent evidence of the old railway is near Greystead Bridge and Thorneyburn Station, which closed in 1956 when the line ceased operation.

Walking north from the Tyne into the eastern edges of Kielder Forest, an area known as Sidwood Forest, is where a journey to the Northumbrian Iron Age and medieval times begins. The forest is home to a host of ancient settlements from the Romano-British circular huts (circa AD75-400) at the start of the trail, through to the substantial bastle house at Black Middens on the eastern side of Tarset Burn.

Of the five bastles visited (the term bastle comes from the French *bastille*, meaning a fortified building), the most substantial and well preserved is Black Middens. It's a fine example of a bastle house, showing how cattle would be held on the ground floor while the family lived above in an elevated stronghold. The lawless and dangerous nature of the bloody borderlands meant that properties like these were essential if a family were to survive.

From the Tarset Bastle Trail the burn leads back towards Greenhaugh and its 300-year-old hostelry, the Holly Bush Inn.

BORDER REIVERS & TARSET BURN

DISTANCE: 17.7KM/11MILES » **TOTAL ASCENT:** 406M/1,332FT » **START GR:** NY 795873 » **TIME:** ALLOW 6.5 HOURS
SATNAV: NE48 1PW » **MAP:** OS EXPLORER OL42, KIELDER WATER & FOREST, 1:25,000 » **REFRESHMENTS:** HOLLY BUSH INN, GREENHAUGH, OR CARRIAGES TEA ROOM, BELLINGHAM » **NAVIGATION:** STRAIGHTFORWARD ON WAYMARKED TRAILS. TAKE CARE ON SECTIONS LINKING THE RIVER TYNE TRAIL AND TARSET BASTLE TRAIL.

Directions – Border Reivers & Tarset Burn

⮕ **Walk south** on the road out of the village, passing a phone box on your right. **Turn right** at a signpost for *High Boughthill ¾*. The track heads downhill initially following Greenhaugh Burn on your right. Upon sight of a ford over Tarset Burn **turn left** (signed *Public Footpath*) and take the bridge and boardwalk ahead. Follow the woodland track next to the river. The path goes past a house on your left and through a number of fields and gates. Upon sight of Redmire House **bear left towards the house** and pass through the two gates to reach the road. **Turn right**, joining the River Tyne Trail, and follow the road uphill to a cattle grid.

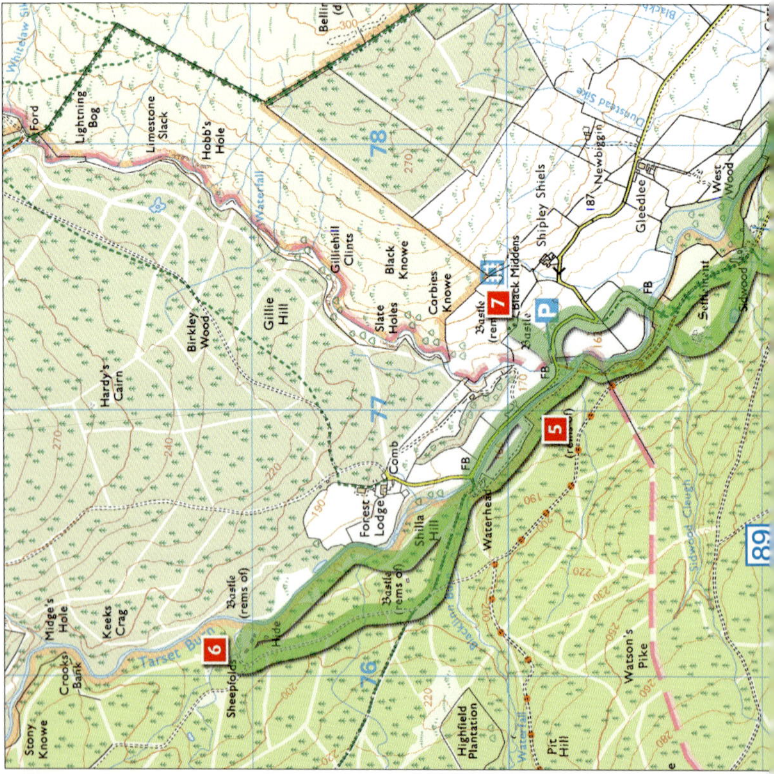

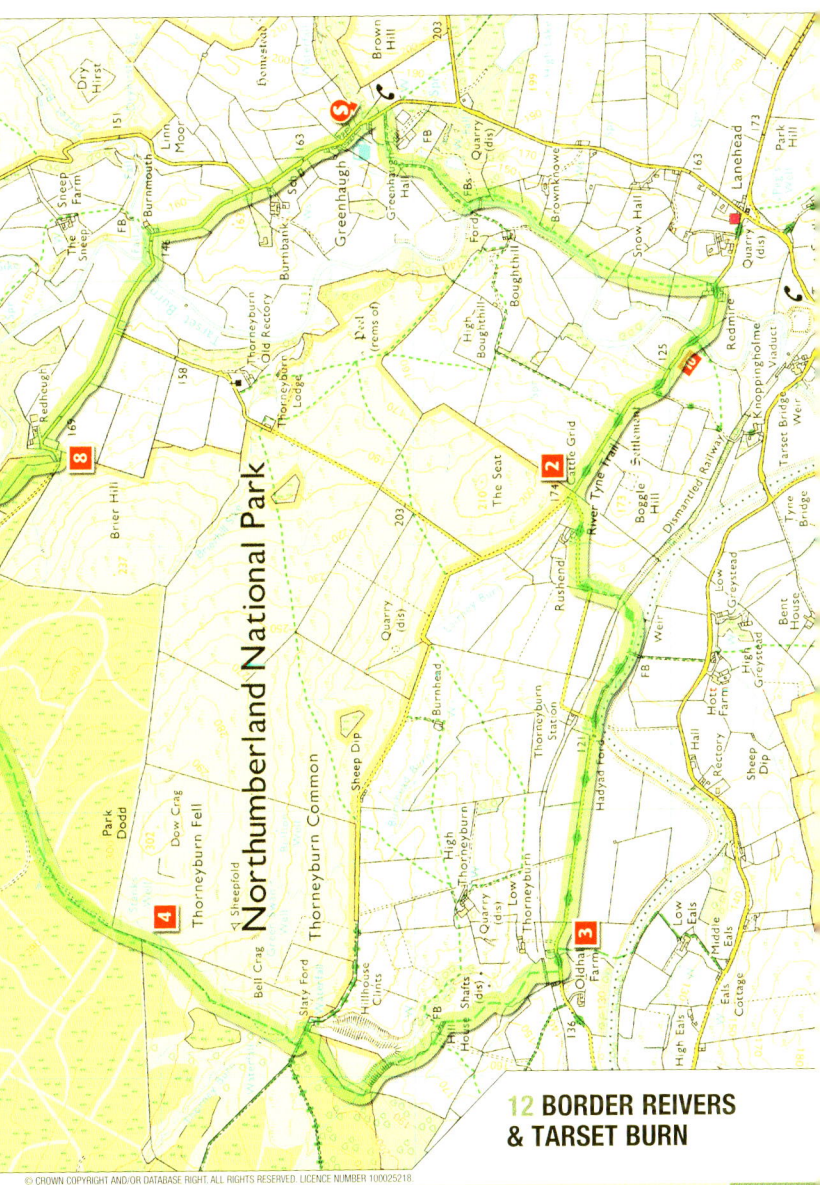

12 BORDER REIVERS & TARSET BURN

Directions – Border Reivers & Tarset Burn continued...

2 Once across the cattle grid **turn left** along a road, heading downhill. Where the road bends to the right go straight ahead over a stile (signed *The Hott ½*), staying on the River Tyne Trail. As you approach an old railway embankment look for an **underpass to the left-hand side**. Stay to the right-hand side of the bank and at a fence line drop down to the entrance and go through the underpass. On exit, the River North Tyne is ahead; bear right and follow the river (on your left) passing Greystead Bridge. Continue along a fence to meet a road. Looking right up the road is Thorneyburn Station; **turn left** to follow our route. Walk until you reach Thorneyburn Cottage.

3 After the cottage, look out for a **gate on the right** signed *Slaty Ford 1*; go through the gate and enter the field. Walk to and go through another gate, then **stay on the left-hand track** to reach Hill House – the exit gate sits at the left corner of the property. **Go through the exit gate, turn left,** and follow the track to a set of small steps on the right leading to gates ahead. On the right is Hillhouse Clints; the path goes around the left-hand side of the fence line. On passing through the gates continue to a large wooden gate and a sign for *Hill House ½* (pointing back in the opposite direction). **Turn left** along a track; shortly afterwards **turn right** (signed *Sidwood 1½*) on a path across heather moorland to reach a dry stone wall. At the right-hand corner of a wall **go through a gate** and enter Sidwood Forest.

4 **Follow a fence for around 100m**; when the fence turns to the right **keep straight ahead** on the forest track. Heading downhill, with trees only on the left initially, stay on the forest track – passing over two gravel roads. Continue downhill through woodland, cross a small burn and eventually reach a road. **Turn left along the road**; at a sign for *Tarset Bastle Trail* **turn left** (the trail is well signed). Follow the trail past a large pond on your left and through the former Iron Age settlement. Upon reaching Sidwood Cleugh **turn right and head downhill**. Cross the forest road and follow a sign for *Black Middens, Hill House & Waterhead*. On reaching Tarset Burn follow a sign for *Hill House & Waterhead*. With the burn on your right you'll pass Hill House Bastle and then **bear right** down steps to the burn.

5 The path leads along the left-hand side of the Waterhead site and to a bridge/ford. **Cross the bridge and turn left at the road** and head up track signed for *Shilla Hill & Boghead*. Continue on the forest track; **turn right** (signed *Boghead*), then **turn right** again (signed *Boghead*) – ahead is a clearing and Boghead Bastle.

6 Pass Boghead Bastle on your left and **follow the trail into woodland**. The trail goes uphill and **curves to the right** to a clearing and Shilla Hill Bastle. Past Shilla Hill, follow the track to reach the forest road again and head downhill to Waterhead. Past Waterhead head towards the main road away from the burn; **turn right along the road**. Follow the road for 500m until it bears left to the car park; **turn left** and walk to Black Middens Bastle.

7 **Retrace your steps** to the road; **turn left** and walk along the road. At a sharp left-hand bend **go through a gate on the right** signed *Tarset Bastle Trail & Sidwood Parking*. The track goes straight ahead and around a field to meet a footbridge. **Cross the footbridge** then take the track heading uphill to meet a forest road. **Turn left** and head towards Sidwood House. From the information board next to the house, follow the grass track beyond into trees and adjacent to the burn. Once past the disused footbridge follow the white/orange arrow signs uphill to reach the road.

8 **Turn left** along the road and begin the walk back to Greenhaugh. Walk past Redheugh House and note the permissive path on your right to the dovecote in field. Stay on the road past Burnmouth House and continue on all the way back to Greenhaugh.

BOGHEAD BASTLE

SECTION 3

History & Heritage

Rich and rewarding trails await those who walk in the footsteps of industrial pioneers and hardy Northumbrians who built this great county.

While these walks celebrate the history and heritage of Northumberland, they also visit some of the most unique natural environments in England, from the hunting estates of Northumbrian royalty to one of the largest man-made forests in Europe.

KIELDER WATER

LAMBLEY VIADUCT. PHOTO: DAVE HEAD/SHUTTERSTOCK.COM

SILVAS CAPITALIS

13 Kielder Water North Shore 22.5km/14miles

Explore the north shore of Northern Europe's biggest man-made lake and the surrounding woodland. A serene trail which also features a range of art and architectural installations.

Kielder Viaduct » Bakethin Reservoir » Silvas Capitalis » Janus Chairs » Plashetts Incline » Belvedere » Robin's Hut » Viewpoints » Kielder Viaduct

Start
Bakethin car park, south of Kielder Village (parking charge). GR: NY 631927.

The Walk
Kielder Water and Forest Park offers a special experience for walkers, and this exploration of the north shore is something unique. In the last century this landscape has transformed from open moorland and native forest to one of Europe's largest man-made reservoirs and woodlands. The walk follows the north shore of Kielder Water, offering discoveries old and new. From a prehistoric beach to remnants of heavy industry, the walk also steps into the modern world through the Kielder Art & Architecture Trail.

The trail is predominantly a level and well-maintained track following an often craggy and eroded shoreline. It begins with views from Kielder Viaduct, which in the nineteenth century carried the Border Counties Railway – a route which still has remnants along Lakeside Way.

Beyond Bakethin Weir, and at the start of Kielder Water, the trail of modern installations begins with Silvas Capitalis (forest head) being the first. This huge wooden head is designed to allow the occupier to listen and look at the surrounding life in the forest. There are a number of other equally fascinating features along the trail, each exploring different interactions and experiences.

The return leg of the walk retraces a number of sections, allowing a different aspect to be viewed given the sun's journey over the sky. Plashetts Incline is a former coal trolley line from the late nineteenth century and follows a track uphill past the location of the former Plashetts Village and miners' terraces.

Kielder Village sits a short walk from Bakethin car park and includes Kielder Castle, which was an eighteenth-century hunting lodge for the Duke of Northumberland (see route 15). The castle is now a visitor centre and cafe.

KIELDER WATER NORTH SHORE
DISTANCE: 22.5KM/14MILES » **TOTAL ASCENT:** 439M/1,440FT » **START GR:** NY 631927 » **TIME:** ALLOW 7 HOURS **SATNAV:** NE48 1HD » **MAP:** OS EXPLORER OL42, KIELDER WATER & FOREST, 1:25,000 » **REFRESHMENTS:** KIELDER CASTLE CAFE, KIELDER » **NAVIGATION:** STRAIGHTFORWARD.

Directions – Kielder Water North Shore

❺▶ Leaving Bakethin car park opposite the car park entrance, take the track uphill on to the viaduct path. **Turn left** at a sign for *Kielder Viaduct*. Walk through trees and over the viaduct – Bakethin Reservoir is on your right. After the viaduct follow the **right-hand grass track** until it rejoins the main track (Lakeside Way). Continue along Lakeside Way passing Bakethin Weir with a view of Kielder Column on the southern shore. Follow a sign for *Kielder Dam 9 Miles*. When you reach a sign for *Silvas Capitalis*, **go into the wood and visit the sculpture**. Return to the main track.

13 KIELDER WATER NORTH SHORE

13 KIELDER WATER NORTH SHORE – **HISTORY & HERITAGE**

Directions – Kielder Water North Shore continued...

2 At a sign for *Kielder Dam 8 miles*, **turn sharp left and head away from the water**. After a brief climb **turn right** and, as you head downhill, rejoin **Lakeside Way** on your right. **Cross a footbridge and take the right-hand track**; continue on and follow a sign to *Janus Chairs*. After visiting the chairs return to the main track.

3 Continue along Lakeside Way, passing the Salmon Cubes installation and on to Plashetts Incline (a slipway). **From the slipway walk all the way up the former coal trolley track,** taking you up the hill and off Lakeside Way. At the top of the incline **continue forward on to a gravel track**. As the track curves left passing Soney Gap (water), **turn right** on to a footpath through trees to return to the edge of the water.

4 **Turn right and follow Lakeside Way,** now heading back towards Bakethin. After 1.2km **turn left** to view the 55/02 installation. **Retrace your steps** to Lakeside Way and **turn left** to continue. A short walk from 55/02 brings you to Belvedere installation and ferry slipway (summer only).

5 As you leave Belvedere there are views behind of Kielder Dam and the Valve Tower. **Continue along Lakeside Way** passing Robin's Hut, which offers a viewpoint across the reservoir to Freya's Hut on the other side. Before you reach Plashetts Incline take the time to **explore the prehistoric beach** (accessed by a left turn down to the shore).

6 From Plashetts Incline rejoin the outward route, following signs for *Kielder Castle*. Cross the footbridge and after a brief climb arrive at a path junction.

7 **Follow Lakeside Way as it bears left into trees** (leaving the outward route). Visit the Viewpoints installation. **Return to Lakeside Way** (with the reservoir on your left) and walk all the way back to Bakethin. Once past Bakethin Weir **turn left** (following *Kielder Village*) and walk over Kielder Viaduct. Once over the viaduct **turn right** at the end of the track to return to the car park.

SALTERS NICK

14 Bolam Lake & Shaftoe Crags

14km/8.7miles

A leisurely walk from the popular Bolam Lake Country Park, through Northumberland farmland and visiting historic settlements. A great walk for both nature and history lovers alike.

Bolam Lake Country Park » Shortflatt Tower » Toft Hill » Shaftoe Crags » Middleton Bridge » River Wansbeck » Bolam Lake Country Park

Start

Boathouse Wood car park, Bolam Lake Country Park (parking charge; the car park is locked at dusk). GR: NZ 083820.

The Walk

Bolam Lake Country Park, with its lakeside path and woodland trails, is a perfect starting point for this walk. For 200 years it's been home to a range of wildlife including swans, red squirrels and roe deer. Less explored are the trails around Bolam which take in Northumberland's farming heartland, historical hidden gems and the early run of one of the county's main rivers; the Wansbeck.

Starting by the cafe, the walk takes in the eastern side of the lake and its nineteenth-century water pump and sluice gate. Upon leaving the country park the walk moves on to farmland, passing through gently rolling fields and farmsteads.

With Shaftoe Crags on the horizon, the route crosses the course of the Devil's Causeway (a Roman road) and on to a cobbled track to the crags. The crags are home to the Devil's Punchbowl (a link back to the causeway?) – an enlarged natural bowl on top of the main sandstone boulder, once filled with wine for the wedding of Sir William Blackett in 1725. Leaving the crags we quickly reach Salters Nick, a dramatic gap in the sandstone and former salt smuggling road into Scotland.

North of Salters Nick, and following the ancient drove road, we visit a standing stone dating back to the Bronze Age and once a place of ceremonial importance.

Back into 'modern' times we pass Middleton South Farm and their rigg and furrow field systems. These are ridges in the land created from ploughing during the Middle Ages.

The final part of the walk crosses the River Wansbeck and passes former medieval settlements, before a short climb to cross the Devil's Causeway and back to Bolam Lake Country Park.

BOLAM LAKE & SHAFTOE CRAGS

DISTANCE: 14KM/8.7MILES » **TOTAL ASCENT:** 215M/705FT » **START GR:** NZ 083820 » **TIME:** ALLOW 4.5 HOURS **SATNAV:** NE20 0HE » **MAP:** OS EXPLORER OL42, KIELDER WATER & FOREST, 1:25,000 » **REFRESHMENTS:** BOLAM LAKE CAFE (CHECK WINTER OPENING TIMES); BLACKSMITHS COFFEE SHOP, BELSAY » **NAVIGATION:** STRAIGHTFORWARD – ROUTE FOLLOWS SIGNED PATHS AND BRIDLEWAYS.

Directions – Bolam Lake & Shaftoe Crags

1 Leaving the car park from the cafe end, **turn left and head downhill** past the information boards and towards the lake. Walk past the old water pump, and **continue ahead** to reach an opening in the trees. Follow the **left-hand path** to Low House Wood car park; leave the car park and **turn right** on to the road. Walk for 100m to reach a T-junction with the main road. **Cross the main road and turn left.** Just after Bolam Low House **turn right** through a kissing gate signed *Harnham 1 mile*.

2 **Enter the field** and head downhill towards the corner to a kissing gate and a small wooden bridge over a burn. **Continue in the same direction** towards trees and a gate opposite. Once through the gate, head along a stone track until you reach the burn and a *Private* sign; **turn right into trees and over a bridge** to meet a gravel farm track. **Turn right** and walk along the track. As the track bears left, **turn right** over a stile and wooden walkway to cross the burn. **Walk for 200m** in the direction shown by the public bridleway sign marked *Sandyford*, towards the farmhouse across the field.

3 Upon meeting a tarmac road, **continue straight ahead** with the farmhouse on your right. Adjacent to the farmhouse pass through a metal gate then, after 200m, cross a bridge over How Burn, enjoying views of Shaftoe Crags to the right in the distance. **Follow the road** through crop fields (the A696 is visible ahead) until you meet a signpost on the left for *East Shaftoe Hall*.

4 **Turn right into the field** towards East Shaftoe Hall. The track ahead dips where the How Burn crosses your path. **Before the gate turn right** and take the bridge over the burn and continue uphill across the field. At this point the track crosses the former Roman road the Devil's Causeway (not visible) and continues towards East Shaftoe Hall. Upon sight of a dry stone wall the track bears right to a gate. **Pass through the gate and take the track towards the hall**; the track heads left (follow *Public Footpath* signs), taking you between the hall and the walled garden. Once past two cottages on your right meet a metal gate.

14 BOLAM LAKE & SHAFTOE CRAGS – HISTORY & HERITAGE

Directions – Bolam Lake & Shaftoe Crags continued...

5 Go through the gate and **follow the cobbled track bearing right up the hill** and past a large oak tree on your right. Enter a section of track with rocky outcrops on both sides and walk for 200m. As the horizon becomes visible you will see a large boulder to your left (Piper's Chair and the Devil's Punchbowl); **turn left and walk for 100m to the boulder**. After exploring the crags **retrace your steps to the main track; turn left along the main track** and continue until you reach Shaftoe Grange House. **Bear right and follow the garden wall** on your left for 350m until you meet a dry stone wall (with a gate) blocking the path. **Turn right** and walk for 100m to explore the Salters Nick area. **Retrace your steps to the gate.**

6 **Go through the gate and turn left** along the tree-lined track. The track passes a small tree plantation on your left, and then goes through **two sets of metal gates**. After **100m, pass through a wooden gate** into a patch of gorse bushes. On the right-hand side of the bushes, **climb over a wall** using stone steps and into a field. Facing forward, **walk in the direction of the house** for 250m (passing a Bronze Age standing stone on your right). **Go through a wooden gate** (marked *Public Footpath*), meet a corner of dry stone wall to your right, and then **follow the walled boundary** of the field until you reach Middleton South Farm. **Go through a gate then turn right** and continue for 50m to reach a wooden gate on your left marked *Public Footpath*.

7 **Go through the gate** and follow the left-hand side of a wall until you reach a gate marked *Public Footpath*. (In the adjacent field to the right you can see the evidence of rigg and furrow farming lines.) **Go through the gate** into a field and **follow the fence along the right-hand side** to reach a patch of trees. **At the trees bear left** away from the fence and walk to the right of a dry stone enclosure towards Middleton Bridge and the main road. The track dips down through gorse and over a burn before rising to reach a gate at the roadside. Go through the gate and **turn left** along the road to reach Middleton Bridge. (On both sides of road are sites of former medieval settlements.)

8 **Cross the bridge and immediately turn right**, signed *Middleton Mill Farm*, and continue along the track to reach the farm. (There are further views to the right of medieval settlements.) Continue **through farm buildings** and through a metal gate. **Bear right** to the corner of the farmyard and **go through a gate** into a field. With the river to your right walk to the gate at the rear of this small field. **Go through**

the gate then turn left and continue for a few metres to reach a cleared track though crops on your right. Take this track and pass through the field; go through the next gate and continue on through a further field. Go through the next gate (marked *Public Bridleway*) and continue in the same direction towards the corner of a fence line to the right. There are a number of wooden walkways over the burn. After crossing the burn **follow the line of burn in the direction of the house** ahead; go through a metal gate in a stone wall then walk ahead through a second gate and **towards a wooden bridge**.

9 **Cross the bridge** and walk towards the **right-hand side of farm buildings** heading towards a gate at a corner of a field. Go through the gate, and with wall/fence line on your left, continue uphill to reach a metal gate leading on to a tarmac road. (This metal gate is the second point where the route crosses the Devil's Causeway.) **Follow the road over two cattle grids** and on to a short climb past Angertonmoor Cottage. Walk for 200m after the cottage to arrive at the main road.

10 **Turn right and walk along the road.** At a junction on your left for Whalton/Bolam **enter Bolam Lake Country Park on the right**. The woodland track then bears left to return to the car park.

BOLAM LAKE COUNTRY PARK

BRIZLEE TOWER

15 Alnwick Castle Estate

13.5km/8.4miles

A leisurely all-weather walk around Hulne Park – the Duke of Northumberland's estate. The only remaining one of Alnwick Castle's parks, it features an eighteenth-century viewing tower and a priory.

Bailiffgate » Hulne Park » Nine Year Aud Hole » Brizlee Tower » Hulne Priory » Duchess's Bridge » Bailiffgate

Start

Bailiffgate Museum & Gallery, Alnwick. GR: NU 185136. Various car parks in Alnwick. Hulne Park is open between 11.00 a.m. and sunset (see www.northumberlandestates.co.uk for planned closures); no dogs are permitted.

The Walk

Alnwick is home to the twelfth Duke of Northumberland (Ralph Percy); the Percy family have owned Alnwick Castle for over 700 years. The second largest inhabited castle in England, it previously boasted a number of parks around its walls, with Hulne Park now the only one remaining.

Over the centuries the park was a recreation and hunting ground for the family and they've hosted many royal visitors, including Princess Margaret (daughter of Henry VII) who was on her way to her wedding in Scotland. While still used for sport, Hulne Park has had many other uses over the years with coal, stone, timber and lime all being taken from the landscape.

These works all had an impact on the land, although today's visitor would not immediately notice this as they wander the well-managed parks and woodlands.

The River Aln cuts through the park, which offers a variety of places to visit. Brizlee Tower, built in 1781, is a striking lookout tower on top of Brizlee Hill. Near the tower is the Nine Year Aud Hole, a hidden cave guarded by a statue of a White Friar. The White Friars, or Carmelites, occupied a special place in Hulne Park where they built their priory in the thirteenth century. Hulne Priory, along with its many related buildings, still sits within a protective wall on top of a green hill looking over the River Aln.

Hulne Park is a perfect walk throughout the seasons. Its metalled roads and solid tracks ensure an accessible all-weather walk, which sits on the outskirts of one of Northumberland's finest towns.

ALNWICK CASTLE ESTATE

DISTANCE: 13.5KM/8.4MILES » **TOTAL ASCENT:** 290M/951FT » **START GR:** NU 185136 » **TIME:** ALLOW 4 HOURS
SATNAV: NE66 1LX » **MAP:** OS EXPLORER 332, ALNWICK & AMBLE, 1:25,000 » **REFRESHMENTS:** THE DIRTY BOTTLES AND VARIOUS CAFES AND PUBS IN ALNWICK » **NAVIGATION:** STRAIGHTFORWARD.

Directions – Alnwick Castle Estate

⮕ From Bailiffgate Museum & Gallery **walk along Bailiffgate** – away from Alnwick Castle – and on to Ratten Row which leads into Hulne Park. **Go through the gatehouse**; stay on the road as it curves to the right and passes over a stone bridge. Stay on the road past Old Moor Lodge and walk **straight ahead** on Farm Drive, which becomes Farm Road.

2 Walk past the entrance to Park Farm and then **turn left** (following the **yellow markers**) to Brizlee Hill. Following the yellow markers, **turn left** to go around the edge of the hill and past Nine Year Aud Hole (a cave), which is guarded by the statue of a White Friar. Continue on the track as it curves around to the right to reach Brizlee Tower. To leave Brizlee Hill, follow the path ahead which drops back down to Farm Road.

3 **Turn left** along Farm Road (following the **blue markers**) – there are views of Hulne Priory to your right – and continue ahead, passing a house at East Brizlee and on to East Brizlee Bridge. **Cross the bridge, immediately turn right, and then cross the Shipley Burn** to join a track. Continue straight ahead to reach Iron Bridge; do not cross the bridge – stay on the track as it curves to the left to face Hulne Priory. **Take the left-hand grass track**, heading uphill to the priory entrance. Explore the church, sacristy and former infirmary before leaving via a gate in the rear wall.

4 **Turn right** out of Hulne Priory and take the track leading through a gate/cattle grid. **Turn right** (following the **blue and red markers**) to reach the river; follow the track past Lady's Well to reach a bridge over a weir.

5 **Turn right and cross the bridge**, then follow the river (on your left) past Monk's Bridge and Duchess's Bridge. At a road junction **turn right** and go up a steady incline to reach Old Moor Lodge again. **Turn left** and follow the outward route over the stone bridge and along Farm Drive and back on to Ratten Row. Go through the gatehouse and return to Bailiffgate.

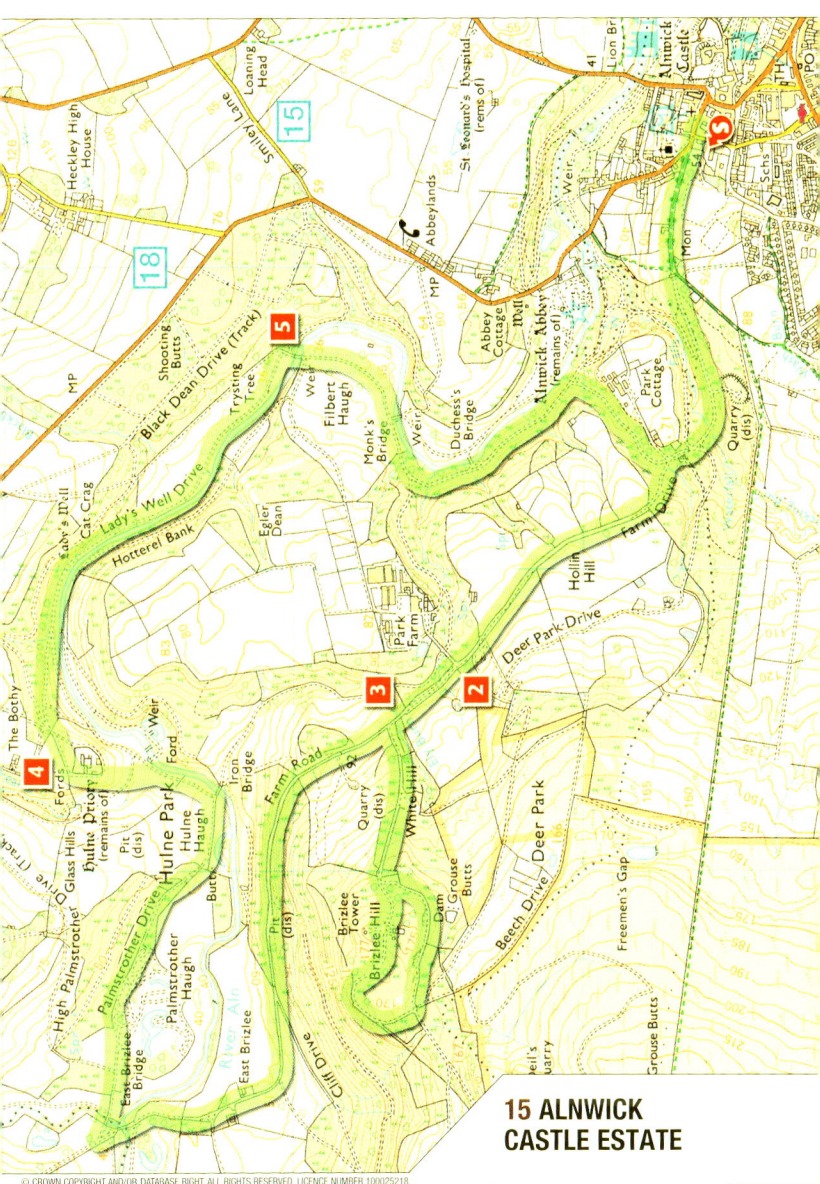

15 ALNWICK CASTLE ESTATE

15 ALNWICK CASTLE ESTATE – HISTORY & HERITAGE

16 Castles of the Tweed & Till 23.2km/14.4miles

From the peaceful spirits of the Duddo Stones, to a castle once known as the most dangerous place in England – the secrets of the River Tweed and the River Till can be discovered on this walk.

Duddo » Duddo Stones » Norham Castle » River Tweed » St Cuthbert's Chapel » River Till » Twizel Castle » Duddo

Start
Duddo Stones parking area (verge parking), west of Duddo. GR: NT 932426.

The Walk
The River Tweed has formed the border between England and Scotland for centuries and the Northumbrian stretch of the river bares all the hallmarks of a turbulent past.

From Berwick-upon-Tweed Castle to Cornhill Castle, the section of the River Tweed running through Northumberland has witnessed border battles like no other place in the country. This was probably the reason why Norham Castle was known as 'the most dangerous place in England' in the fourteenth century. Built two centuries earlier, Norham Castle stood guard over its village and the river against Scottish attacks. It has rarely changed hands with the infamous Battle of Flodden in 1513 being one of those times.

The Battle of Flodden also involved another of this walk's fortifications: Twizel Castle. Originally a medieval tower, in 1513 Twizel Castle was visited by James IV of Scotland on his way to besiege Norham Castle. Over the centuries a number of developments have been tried to improve Twizel Castle but it now stands as a ruinous hidden gem on the River Till.

The border rivers, which would have once run red, are now some of the cleanest waters in the country. Otters, herons, kingfishers and deer thrive in a habitat that is shared with anglers who come to enjoy the salmon-rich waterway.

Despite years of battles this borderland has also served as a proud custodian of one of Northumberland's most unique sites. Surviving millennia of conflict, Duddo Stones stand unassuming in a field at the start of the walk. Believed to have been erected over 4,000 years ago, the five remaining stones are both a spiritual and natural wonder to those that visit.

CASTLES OF THE TWEED & TILL

DISTANCE: 23.2KM/14.4MILES » **TOTAL ASCENT:** 291M/955FT » **START GR:** NT 932426 » **TIME:** ALLOW 7 HOURS
SATNAV: TD15 2PS » **MAP:** OS EXPLORER 339, KELSO, COLDSTREAM & LOWER TWEED VALLEY, 1:25,000
REFRESHMENTS: THE MASONS ARMS, NORHAM » **NAVIGATION:** STRAIGHTFORWARD.

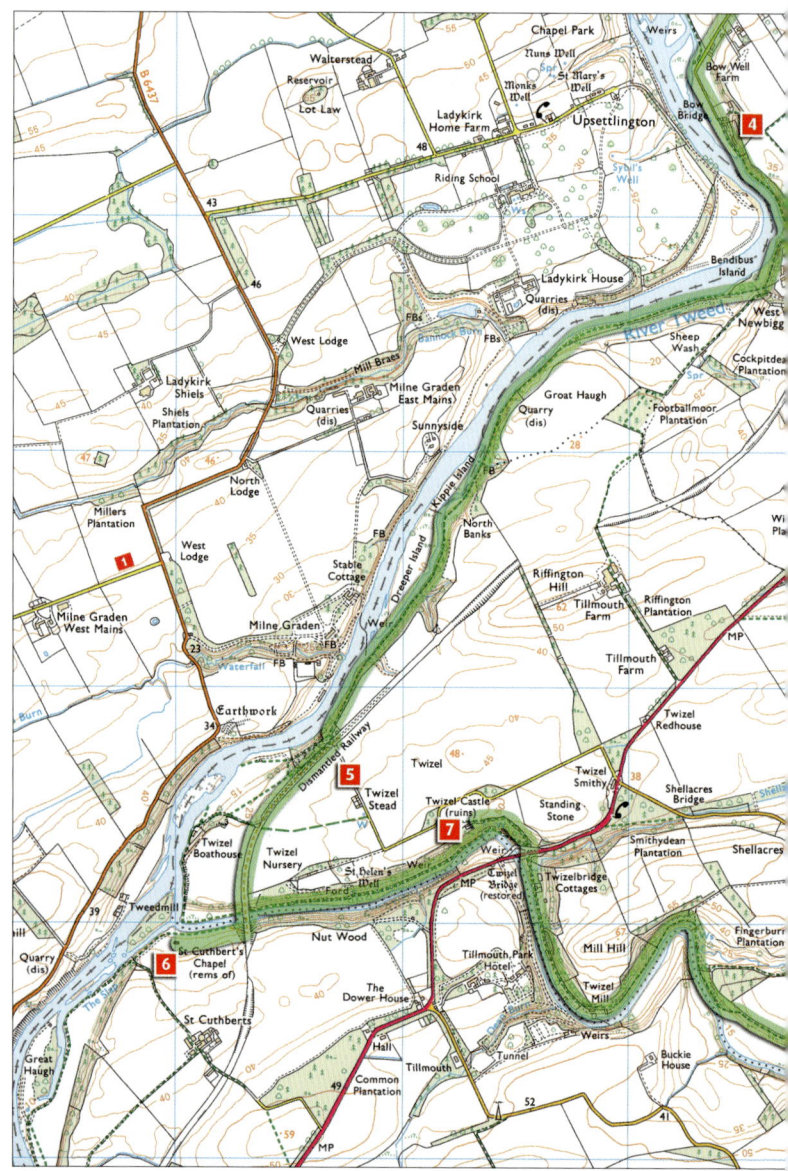

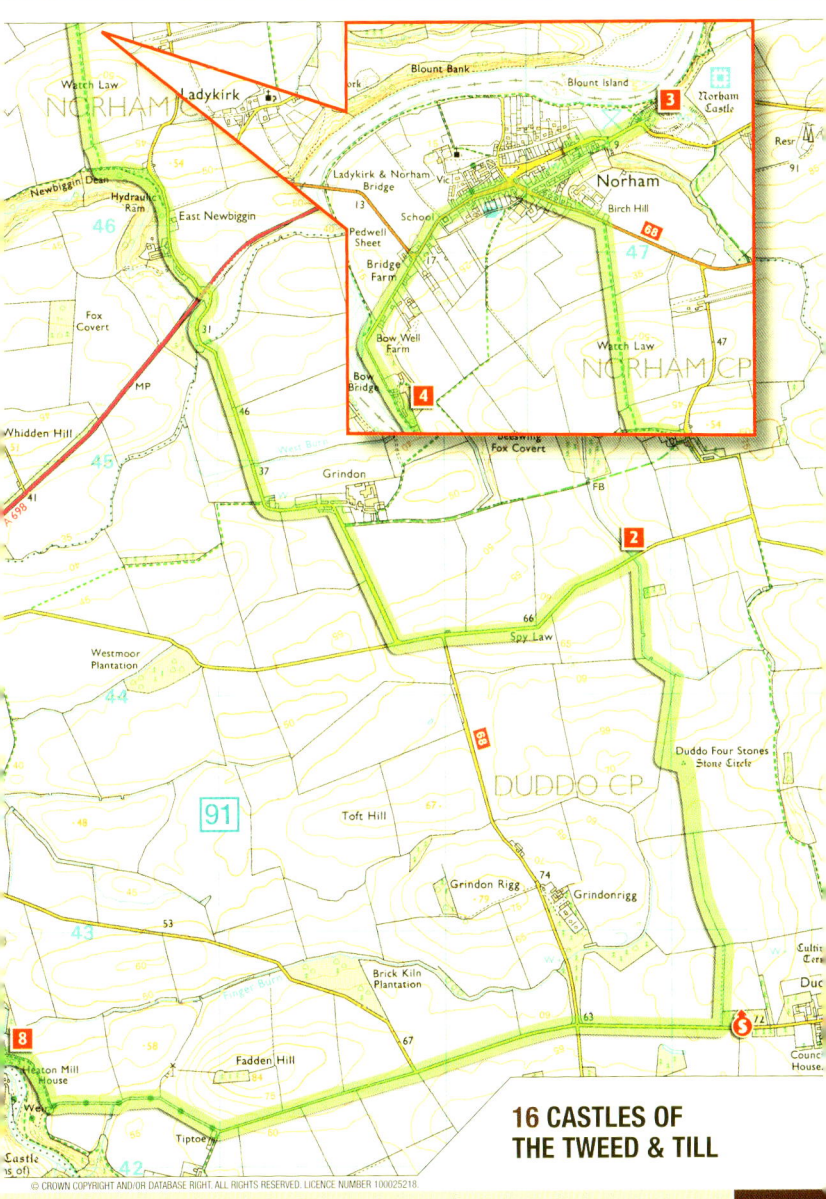

16 CASTLES OF THE TWEED & TILL

Directions – Castles of the Tweed & Till

↪ At the marked field entrance for Duddo Stones **follow permissive paths for 1.1km** through fields to reach the stone circle. To leave the stones take the permissive path to the interpretation board at the edge of the field. **Turn right** and walk to the corner of a field and a small footbridge. **Cross the footbridge** then **turn left** and follow the field boundary all the way to a gate and the main road.

2 Go through the gate and **turn left on to the main road.** Go straight ahead at the next junction then **turn right** (following the sign for *Grindon ½*). **Walk into Grindon** and follow the road as it curves to the left past houses. Continue on the road until you reach the A698. **Cross the A698 and turn left.** Then **immediately turn right** along a road (following the sign for *Norham 1¼*). Walk through East Newbiggin then **turn left** through a gate (following the sign for *West Newbiggin 1*). Walk along the track until you reach a signpost for *Norham ¾*. **Turn right** here; the trail follows the right-hand side of a field to reach a road. **Turn left** and follow the road into Norham. **Turn right** along South Lane then, at the end of the road, **turn left** along a small track leading to Castle Street. **Turn right** and walk to Norham Castle.

3 After exploring the castle **retrace your steps** back towards the village. Continue along Castle Street then turn right along West Street. At the far end of the village, where the main road curves to the right, **turn left** (following the sign for *Boathouse and Norham Dene*) to reach the River Tweed and a gate with a signpost for *Twizel Bridge 4 miles*.

4 **Follow the track along the River Tweed** then **turn right** at a track junction and go over a footbridge. Continue to **keep right on the track and follow the river**. The trail sits close to the bank and goes past Fishermans' huts until it climbs slightly, past a seating area, to a house sitting above the river.

5 **Walk around to the rear of the house** to a signpost sitting on the former Tweedmouth–Kelso railway line. **Turn right** to follow the permissive path signed *Twizel Viaduct ½*. Walk across the viaduct then **turn right** at a fingerpost for *Tweed Riverbank Path ¼*. This path drops down to the river and into a field to visit the ruins of St Cuthbert's Chapel.

6 After visiting the chapel **retrace your steps across the viaduct** then **turn right** towards the river. The descent to the river is steep and can be slippery at times. Follow the safest route down to meet the footpath and **turn left** (the River Till is on your right). Continue along the footpath until you reach a signpost for *Castle ¼* (you can see Twizel Bridge up ahead). **Turn left** here and follow the track the uphill to Twizel Castle.

7 After exploring the castle **retrace your steps to the river.** Go through a metal gate, with Twizel Bridge on your right, then cross over the A698 and **continue straight ahead on to a track** (following the sign for *Etal 5½*). Along the track is Twizel Mill, where the path curves to the left uphill. **Follow the line of the river** and pass through a gate and over a wooden bridge. Keeping next to river pass through a gate and follow the base of hill to a signpost for *Landslip on Riverside Path Rejoin in ¼ mile*. Follow sign direction uphill to the gate.

8 At the gate do not follow temporary stiles to the right as these lead to an overgrown path with steep crags to the right. **Go through the gate, turn right,** and follow the fence/wall to a gate. Go through the gate and continue on (the track sits high above the river with views across to Heaton Castle). Go over a stile and reach a signpost for *River Till and Etal 4*. **Turn left** here and follow the grass track between hedgerows to reach the main road at the hamlet of Tiptoe. **Turn left** and follow the road to return to the start.

DUDDO STONES

BOTHAL CASTLE

17 Morpeth & River Wansbeck

12.2km/7.6miles

A simple river walk from one of Northumberland's busiest market towns. The river and woodland trail has been popular since Victorian times.

Morpeth Chantry » River Wansbeck » Stephenson's Viaduct » Lady Chapel » Bothal » Parish Haugh » Carlisle Park » Morpeth Chantry

Start

Morpeth Tourist Information Centre, Morpeth Chantry, Bridge Street, Morpeth. Various car parks in Morpeth. GR: NZ 200859.

The Walk

Morpeth has played a central role in Northumbrian history given its status as a market town since the twelfth century. Straddling the River Wansbeck, and once the route of the Great North Road, the town is a popular destination for both locals and tourists.

The name is suggested to originate from 'moor path' – from the land surrounding the town and the former marshes around the site of what is now Carlisle Park.

Carlisle Park is now home to not only well-groomed gardens, but also to the gatehouse of Morpeth Castle, a garden in memory of the town's son and botanist William Turner, and a statue of Emily Davison – the English suffragette who died in 1913 fighting for votes for woman. Davison is now buried nearby in St Mary's Churchyard.

On the edge of town we follow a stretch of the River Wansbeck that is rich in natural and industrial history. The river walk is home to a range of birdlife as well as animals such as badgers and foxes. The natural inhabitants here now wouldn't always have been present given the historic industries in the area. The section of river along to Bothal Castle had coal mines, a quarry (providing stone for the castle, viaduct and many local buildings) and was a thoroughfare for those working in the area. The popularity of the route also gave rise to the now ruinous Lady Chapel and associated well.

Morpeth Chantry, sitting at the end of the town's footbridge and concluding this walk, served as a toll house collecting pontage (tolls) from those entering the town. It now houses Morpeth Bagpipe Museum and Morpeth Tourist Information Centre.

MORPETH & RIVER WANSBECK

DISTANCE: 12.2KM/7.6MILES » **TOTAL ASCENT:** 184M/604FT » **START GR:** NZ 200859 » **TIME:** ALLOW 4 HOURS **SATNAV:** NE61 1PD » **MAP:** OS EXPLORER 325, MORPETH & BLYTH, 1:25,000 » **REFRESHMENTS:** THE CHANTRY TEA ROOMS, MORPETH » **NAVIGATION:** STRAIGHTFORWARD.

Directions – Morpeth & River Wansbeck

- From Morpeth Chantry walk east along Bridge Street, past St George's Church. Go straight on at two roundabouts. Passing the supermarket, **turn right (going down steps)**, leading down below the car park to a burn. Walk alongside the burn then continue straight ahead to walk alongside the River Wansbeck, eventually meeting a road. **Cross the main road. Turn right** and walk along the large lay-by then **turn left (up steps)** to enter Bluebell Woods. Follow the track ahead. **Take the right-hand track** at a signpost for *1 Cottingwood*; then **turn right** (signed for *Bothal 2½*) to meet the main road.

2 **Cross the road** – which can be very busy – and **join the river trail** straight ahead. After 750m pass under Stephenson's Viaduct. Beyond the viaduct continue for 1km reach Chapel Wood. In Chapel Wood pass a picnic area, Victorian well and the remains of Lady Chapel. Continue on to the remains of a 400-year-old weir.

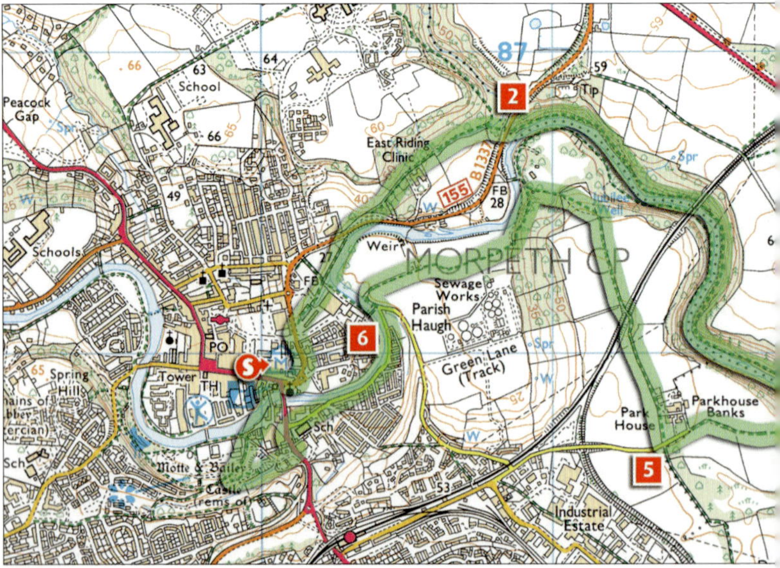

3 From the weir continue to a small car park next to a disused sawmill. Continue on to reach a road; **turn left** along the road then **turn right** along the main road. Follow the road – with views of Bothal Castle to your right – all the way into Bothal. In Bothal **turn right at the church**; once past it follow the sign for *River Wansbeck*. The grass track takes you down to the riverside. On reaching the water **turn right and take the stepping stones** to the other side*. (The bridge above is private and used by the church.) Follow the track as it rises above the river and **continue straight ahead to join a tarmac road** (between two posts). When the **road curves to the left, turn right** on to a track into a field. Briefly follow the field edge to your right and exit via an opening into trees. After a short distance the trail heads off to right and drops down to the bank to a road. At the road **turn left and follow the road uphill.**

*If the river level is higher than the stepping stones, retrace your steps back to the small car park next to the disused sawmill. Turn left over the bridge and walk uphill to rejoin the route.

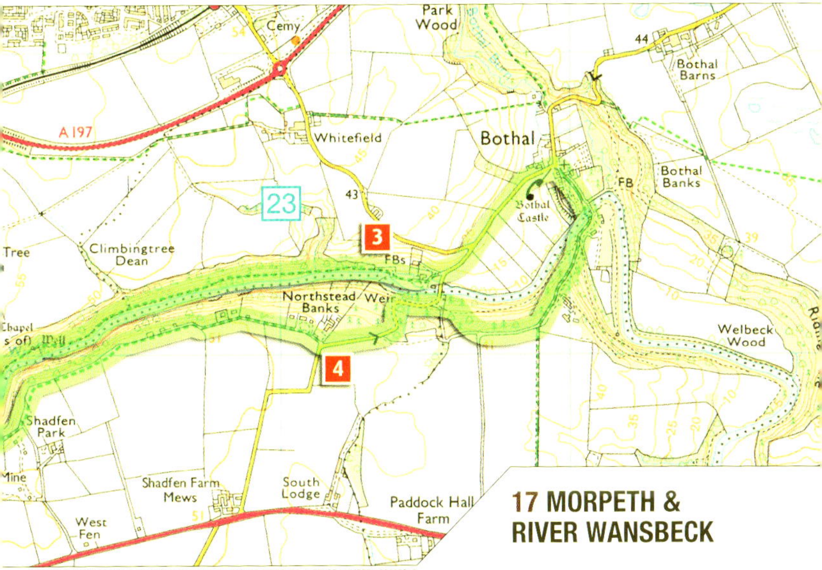

17 MORPETH & RIVER WANSBECK

Directions – Morpeth & River Wansbeck continued…

4 When you reach a *Private Road* sign on a bend, **turn right** (following the sign for *Park House 1¼*), which takes you along the edge of various fields – sometimes passing through hedgerows – until the track drops down into trees and a former coal mine. **Cross the burn** via a bridge and walk up the steps. **Turn right at the top of the steps** and continue on the track heading out of the trees. Continue heading towards houses (the track sits between two fields). At the houses briefly **join a farm road** before arriving at a junction.

5 **Turn right** along a track for *Whorral Bank ¾*. The track goes over a railway bridge and into a field. Follow the track along the field dropping into trees to reach a metal bridge over the River Wansbeck (don't cross the bridge). **Turn left and walk along the river**. The riverside trail continues all the way into edge of town where it meets a road.

6 **Turn right on to the road** – still next to the river – and follow all the way to meet the A192. **Turn left and cross the road then turn right into Carlisle Park**. In the park walk straight ahead toward Haw Hill past the William Turner Garden and the Emily Davison statue. **Walk to the left side of Haw Hill and turn right** to climb over to the other side. **Drop down to the river and turn right**. At the next junction **turn left** to cross Chantry Footbridge bringing you to the rear of Morpeth Chantry and the end of the walk.

VIADUCT OVER THE RIVER WANSBECK

BLACKETT LEVEL

18 Allendale & Isaac's Tea Trail   18.1km/11.2miles

Discover the North Pennines Area of Outstanding Natural Beauty and how the relationship between nature and industry has crafted the landscape.

Allendale Town » Isaac's Tea Trail » Allen Smelt Mill » Keenley Church » Monk Wood » Dryburn Moor » Allendale Chimneys » Bridge End » Allendale Town

Start
Market Place, Allendale Town. Various parking options in Allendale Town. GR: NY 837558.

The Walk
It is advisable not to take dogs on this walk as a section of moorland has restrictions due to nesting birds.

The North Pennines Area of Outstanding Natural Beauty sits on the southern border of Northumberland and is one of the UK's most wild and unique landscapes. Vast expanses of moorland, traditional farming valleys and industrious towns have created an area which is fascinating to those who visit.

It's home to a third of England's upland hay meadows and blanket bogs and has 80 per cent of the country's black grouse population, and all of this from a place which once produced a sixth of Britain's lead.

The natural and industrial influences around Allendale are highlighted on a local trail called Isaac's Tea Trail. This walk follows over ten kilometres of Isaac's Tea Trail, a route walked by Isaac Holden, a famous local tea seller. At the start of the nineteenth century, when he was just eight years old, Isaac worked in lead mining until a decline in the industry forced him into a new career as a roaming tea seller and 'do gooder'. For his commitment to the community he is remembered by this trail and memorial in St Cuthbert's Churchyard.

The lead mining heritage of the area is celebrated at the end of the walk with a journey back to Allendale along an industrial scar across the moorland – the Allendale Chimneys are lasting monuments to an industry which brought wealth and work to a rural region. The chimneys stand at the end of the flues which carried the smoke from Allen Smelt Mill (at the start of the walk) away from the valley. These crumbling flue lines are the 200-year-old guides leading back to the town.

ALLENDALE & ISAAC'S TEA TRAIL
DISTANCE: 18.1KM/11.2MILES » **TOTAL ASCENT:** 497M/1,631FT » **START GR:** NY 837558 » **TIME:** ALLOW 6 HOURS **SATNAV:** NE47 9AZ » **MAP:** OS EXPLORER OL43, HADRIAN'S WALL, 1:25,000 » **REFRESHMENTS:** THE GOLDEN LION OR THE KINGS HEAD, ALLENDALE » **NAVIGATION:** STRAIGHTFORWARD ON ISAAC'S TEA TRAIL; TAKE CARE CROSSING MOORLAND TO JOIN ROAD.

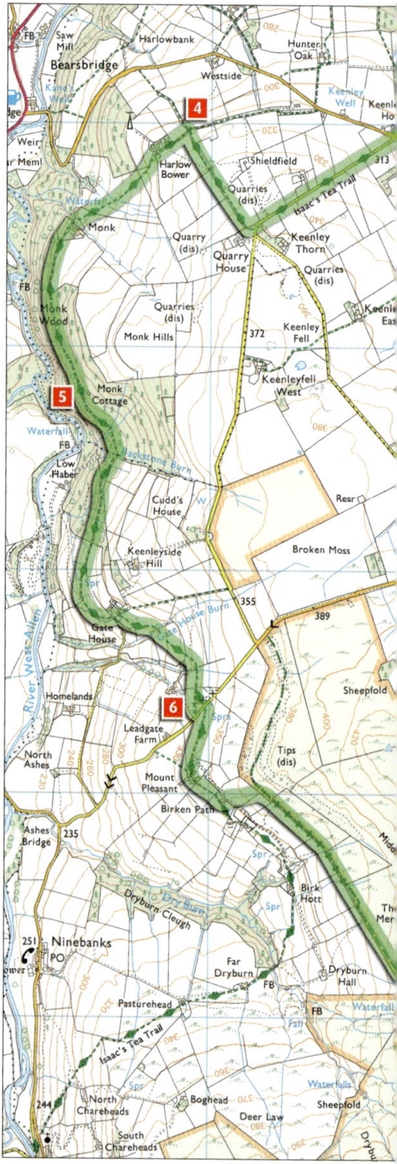

116 DAY WALKS IN NORTHUMBERLAND

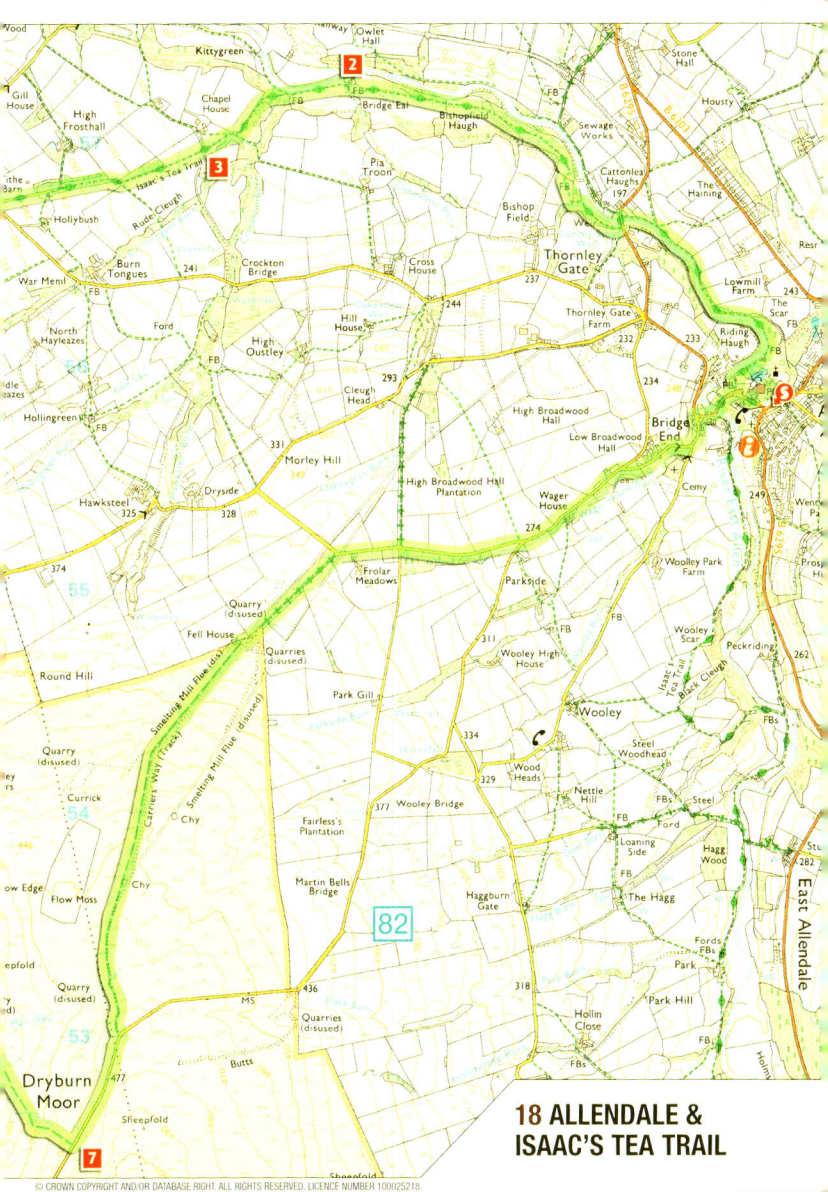

18 ALLENDALE & ISAAC'S TEA TRAIL

18 ALLENDALE & ISAAC'S TEA TRAIL – **HISTORY & HERITAGE**

Directions – Allendale & Isaac's Tea Trail

1 Leave the Market Place past Allendale Forge Studios then **turn right**. Head downhill and **turn right** (following signs for *Allendale Bridge ¾* and *Isaac's Tea Trail*). Follow the path along the river and past Blackett Level. Stay on the path until you reach a road bridge. **Walk over the bridge** (Allen Smelt Mill is on your left) then **turn right** (following signs for *Oakpool 2* and *Isaac's Tea Trail*). Walk along the river – follow the well-signed footpath diversion.

2 When you reach the house at Bridge Eal **follow the path around the wall and briefly into the garden** to cross the bridge. **The trail then heads to the left**, up a steep bank and through a gate. At a post **take the right-hand footpath** and follow to a stile. At a field **take the left-hand track** (heading away from the house) across the field to a fingerpost.

3 Go through the opposite gate – waymarked *Isaac's Tea Trail* – and head to the left-hand side of trees ahead towards a wall. Around to the **rear of the trees turn right** and go over a stile into a tree copse. (On your left is a church and straight ahead is the onward road.) Follow the road to a junction and **turn right**. Follow the road to Keenleywell House and **turn left** (following signs for *Ninebanks*). When the road curves to the left, **go over a stile on the right**, and head down the track to a wall. Continue ahead over a number of stiles to meet a farm road.

4 **Turn left and walk towards the farm**. Walk into the farm and go through a **gate on the right-hand side** of a shed. Follow the wall on your right heading downhill to the corner of a field. Go through a gate, follow telegraph poles towards a house ahead and go through a gate and on to a farm track. On your right is a fingerpost for *Leadgate Bank 1½* and *Isaac's Tea Trail*.

5 Continue on the trail past Monk Cottage and follow what is generally a wide, wooded track. Go through a gate which leads on to a grass track along a wall, going uphill to a further gate and taking a **left turn** up a bank. Go through next gate and **head to the right-hand side towards a wind turbine** and through a gate in a wall. Head towards buildings and pass through a gate. Continue to a stile and keep going to meet a road.

6 Turn left along the road then immediately **turn right** (following a sign for *Mount Pleasant ¼*) and follow the track to houses. Stay on the track to the left of Mount Pleasant Farm and before the next building **turn left on to a quad track**. Cross to the other side of a wall then **turn right**. The track now leads between two stone walls before it reaching open moorland. Continue until you reach the main road.

7 **Turn left** and walk along the road until you reach a small parking area and information board for Allendale Chimneys. **Turn left** on to the clear route past the chimneys and flues down to Fell House. Beyond Fell House continue straight ahead to join a track leading to the main road. **Turn right** and follow the road for 1.4km to a junction. **Turn right** here (on to a single-track road). **Turn left** at the next junction into Bridge End, then **turn right**, walk over a bridge and return to the start.

KEENLEYWELL HOUSE

TRIG POINT ON LONG CRAG

19 Thrunton Wood

12.9km/8miles

A circular walk around one of the Forests of Rothbury (a collection of Northumberland woodlands). This raised forest and moorland offers fine views of the surrounding landscape.

Thrunton Wood car park » Thrunton Crag » Castle Hill » Macartney's Cave » Hob's Nick » Long Crag » Coe Crags Wood » Thrunton Wood car park

Start
Thrunton Wood car park. GR: NU 085097.

The Walk

Thrunton Wood is a mixed use woodland and part of the Forests of Rothbury collection – a group of six Forestry England sites in north-east Northumberland.

While the Forestry Commission has only been established since 1919, woodlands such as Thrunton have a history which is deep in the landscape. Planted on two sandstone escarpments (Thrunton Crag to the north; Long Crag and Coe Crags to the south), the trees hide a network of trails which visit a host of unique sites.

In the north-west corner of Thrunton Wood you'll find Castle Hill – where in the twelfth century the Callaly family began to build a castle, but never finished. Legend has it that the hill was the home of fairies and they opposed the construction of the castle, so each night they would take down all the day's work! Eventually Lord Callay conceded defeat and built his castle in the valley where it stills stands today.

A short walk from Castle Hill is another magical site in the form of Macartney's Cave. This hand hewn work isn't the toil of fairies, but that of a local monk who sought solitude during the nineteenth century. Perhaps from the hobgoblins of Hob's Nick above?

Outside the legends of the forest, the walk follows scars across heather moorland with spectacular views to the north of the Cheviot Hills. While to the south sits the raised trails across Long Crag and Coe Crags. On top of the crags is a prime viewpoint for the varied wildlife in the area, from grazing deer amongst the scrub, to the hovering kestrels which can be seen flying below the vigilant walker.

THRUNTON WOOD

DISTANCE: 12.9KM/8MILES » **TOTAL ASCENT:** 459M/1,506FT » **START GR:** NU 085097 » **TIME:** ALLOW 4.5 HOURS **SATNAV:** NE66 4SG » **MAP:** OS EXPLORER 332, ALNWICK & AMBLE, 1:25,000 » **REFRESHMENTS:** THE RUNNING FOX, LONGFRAMLINGTON » **NAVIGATION:** STRAIGHTFORWARD.

Directions – Thrunton Wood

❺▶ From the car park **turn left** and head north along the road. **Turn left at the first forestry track/gate** before the road drops downhill. Follow the track through forest and past a seating area on your right; after 1.6km meet a small fence on your right.

2 Go round the fence and **turn right on to a track** crossing Thrunton Crag – take care as some sections are steep. The track curves to the left along the tree line before meeting a forestry track. Continue straight ahead on the track, which curves to the right and eventually runs parallel with a dry stone wall on your left. **Turn left through a gate in the wall** then follow the **left-hand track** which climbs steeply and begins to head back in the direction of the crag. Reach a flat plateau of older trees on Castle Hill and explore the former fort.

3 From where you joined Castle Hill look out for nick to the left-hand side and **take the track heading downhill**. The track curves to the left and heads down a natural gully to meet a stile and a steep slope ahead. Go over the stile and continue uphill; look out for Macartney's Cave on the right-hand side. Follow the track beyond the cave continuing uphill to reach the top of Callaly Crag. **Bear right** on to a path which is also used as mountain bike track. The track goes across heather moors, with views of the Cheviot Hills to your right, and the prominent route to a large cairn ahead. Continue to the cairn, from where you can see Long Crag and the Simonside Ridge beyond.

4 Walk away from the cairn towards Long Crag and meet a gate in the fence on your left. **Go through the gate** and head downhill then **go through a kissing gate on your right**. The track then continues downhill. Beyond the next gate the track climbs to the top of Long Crag. Follow the track all the way up – the track curves to the left near the top – to reach the trig point on Long Crag.

5 Leaving the trig point follow the ridge path **keeping to left-hand tracks** all the way across the top of crags. At Coe Crags continue forward; the track eventually curves to the left into Coe Crags Wood. The path levels out – don't drop down a track on the right here. Follow the path for 200m then **turn right on to a track into trees** (quite dark) and follow downhill to a bridge.

6 Cross the bridge and **turn right** on to a forestry track. Follow the track for 1.1km then **bear right** (following signs for *car park*) to reach the road. **Turn left** and walk uphill to reach the car park.

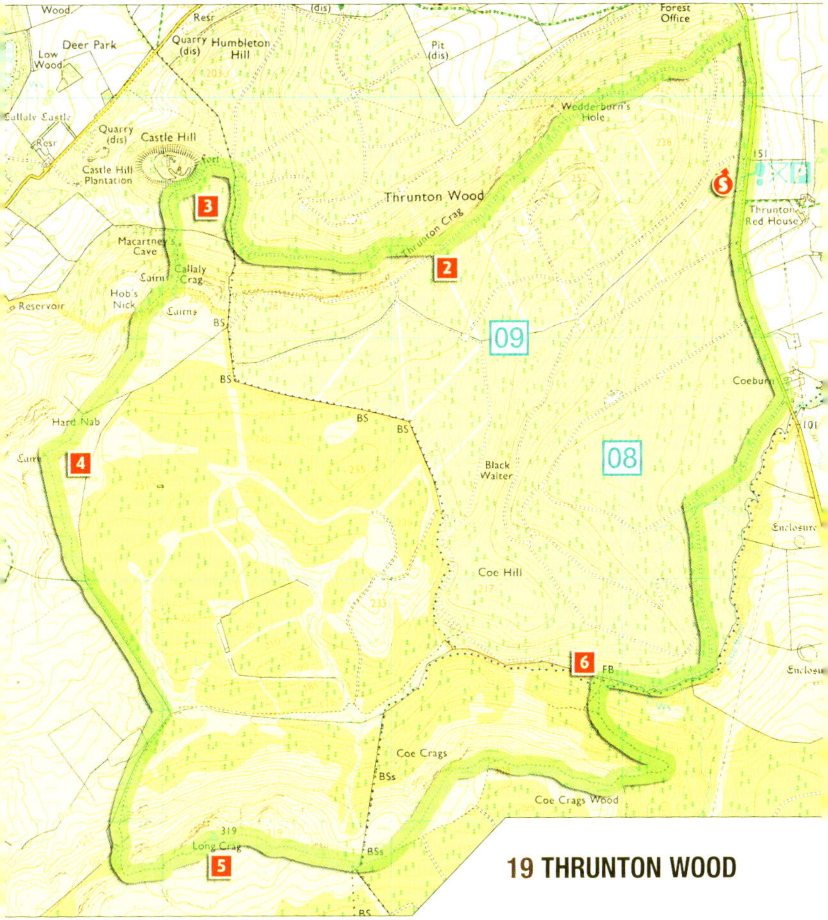

19 THRUNTON WOOD

LAMBLEY VIADUCT

20 River South Tyne & Rails

22.3km/13.9miles

A history and heritage trail exploring the southern boundary of Northumberland, and the river and rails which became the backbone of the landscape.

Featherstone Park » Featherstone Castle » River South Tyne » Lambley Viaduct » Pennine Way » Slaggyford » South Tyne Trail » Lambley Viaduct » Featherstone Park

Start
Featherstone Park car park, Featherstone Rowfoot. GR: NY 682607.

The Walk
The former Alston line, running from Haltwhistle to Alston, opened in 1852 and was part of the Newcastle and Carlisle Railway. It connected the lead mining district of the South Tyne with the main city-to-city route. The line survived the Beeching plan of 1963, but ultimately closed in 1976 when it was thought it would've been cheaper to transport the few remaining regular passengers by a chauffeur-driven Bentley!

The Alston line was one of the finest routes through rural North East England and now benefits from a heritage line operating alongside a fine river trail.

Featherstone Castle sits at the north end of the trail and watches over Camp 18 – a prisoner-of-war camp that housed thousands of German officers during World War II, until it closed in 1948. The remaining buildings of the camp are accessible, albeit now with some resident cattle.

Crossing the River South Tyne under the shadow of the Lambley Viaduct, the completion of which marked the opening of the full branch line, the trail leads to the Pennine Way and former Roman road, the Maiden Way.

Slaggyford is the turning point for the walk, as well as being the terminus for the South Tynedale Railway. The renovated station is a highlight, with its traditional platform and station buildings, and benefitting from a regular service along the narrow-gauge railway. The heritage line sits on the track bed of the old route, and the journey back to Featherstone is along the northern stretch of the line.

A leisurely return walk awaits including fantastic views over the River South Tyne and the chance to walk on top of the previously seen Lambley Viaduct, standing over 30 metres high.

RIVER SOUTH TYNE & RAILS

DISTANCE: 22.3KM/13.9MILES » **TOTAL ASCENT:** 435M/1,427FT » **START GR:** NY 682607 » **TIME:** ALLOW 7 HOURS
SATNAV: NE49 0JF » **MAP:** OS EXPLORER OL43, HADRIAN'S WALL, 1:25,000 » **REFRESHMENTS:** THE WALLACE ARMS, ROWFOOT » **NAVIGATION:** STRAIGHTFORWARD.

Directions – River South Tyne & Rails

S▶ From the car park join the main road. **Turn left** and follow the road past Featherstone Castle to meet the River South Tyne. **Go through a gate and turn left** following the *River Tyne Trail* waymark with the river on your right. The track goes past the castle (now on your left) and meets the old road alongside the ruins of Camp 18, a prisoner-of-war camp. Past Camp 18 the farm track curves to the left to meet a road.

2 **Cross the road** and continue on the River Tyne Trail. Follow the river until the trail **curves to the left** towards Shafthill Farm and briefly away from the river. Go through a gate (following *River Tyne Trail*) and **turn right**, heading back towards the river and the church across the river in Lambley. The trail runs alongside the river again and to a corner of a field through a gate and on to a river/woodland track. Walk until you reach a footbridge. **Cross the footbridge and follow the track** (with the river on your left) to steps and up to a post. **Turn right through a gate** (following the sign for *Lambley ¼*) and at the top walk along steps. Go through a gate to a farm track and continue on to a road.

3 **Turn right** and walk into Lambley. Enjoy views of Whin Sill and Hadrian's Wall to the north-east. Pass the church then shortly afterwards **turn left between buildings**, go through an underpass and across fields to a stile and a road. **Turn left** and walk to a T-junction. **Turn left and cross the road then turn right** on to a track (following a sign for *Burnstones 3*). The route follows the Maiden Way and the Pennine Way. Pass over a number of stiles and meet a dry stone wall. **The trail switches to the other side of the wall** and drops downhill to a stile and a bridge alongside a bend in the main road.

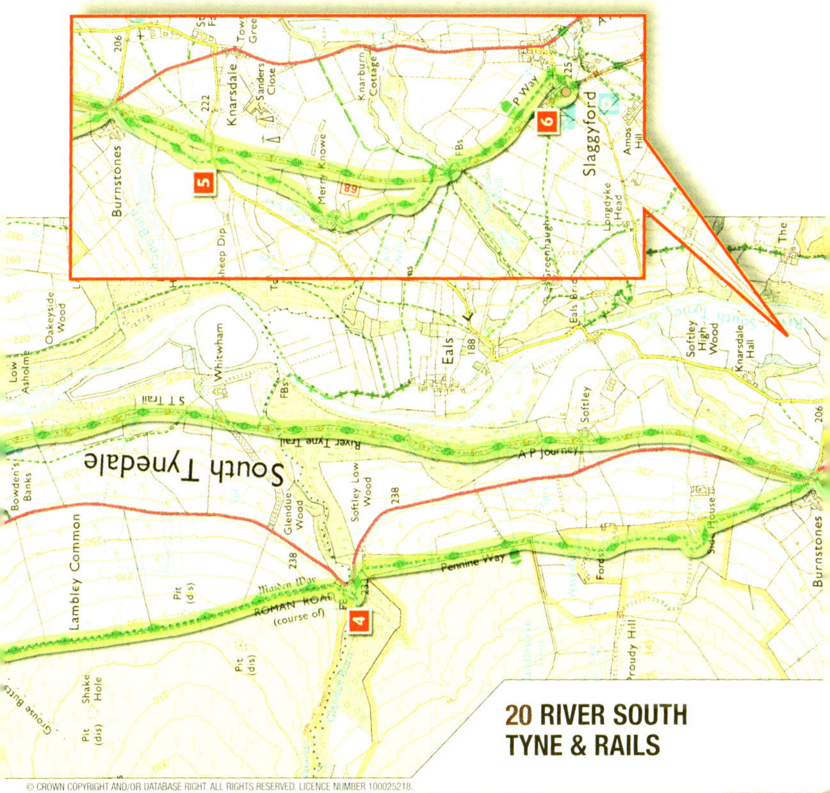

20 RIVER SOUTH TYNE & RAILS

Directions – River South Tyne & Rails continued...

4 **Cross the bridge** then head uphill **bearing right and over a stile**. Continue to follow the Pennine Way alongside a wall. Cross a low-level ford and walk to the *Pennine Way* signpost directing you to **turn left down a farm track**. Continue through a kissing gate to Burnstones. Meet the road and walk straight ahead under a bridge. **After the bridge turn right** (following the sign for *Slaggyford 1½*) and walk under the same bridge again. **Follow the river**, go up steps and through a gate (staying on the Pennine Way). Go straight ahead over stiles to meet a road.

5 **Follow the signpost on the left** for *Slaggyford 1¼*. Follow the trail to a farmhouse and, on the approach, before a metal gate, look for gap in the wall on your left. **Go through the gap** and keep right around the field to wall steps into the yard. Follow homemade *Pennine Way* signs (further steps into another yard taking you ultimately back into a field). Cross the field, head downhill towards the burn and underpass. Once **through the underpass follow the wall line, over the cobbled burn and across a footbridge**. Follow the track, **keeping left when track splits**, and follow all the way into Slaggyford. **Turn right** at the main road and walk up to the station on your right.

6 Leaving the station **retrace your steps** back along the road and behind buildings on the South Tyne Trail and Pennine Way. At a post beyond the train track, follow the signs for *South Tyne Trail* and *River Tyne Trail*. **The route now follows the old railway line all the way back**. The trail has some great views over the River South Tyne on your right. After 6km you will approach a house at Waughold Holme, with views of the viaduct ahead.

7 **Keep left past the house on the South Tyne Trail**. After 100m the track curves to the right downhill and below Station House. **Walk under the viaduct** and up steps to the left. **Midway up the steps turn left at a fingerpost** (following *South Tyne Trail North via Lambley Viaduct*) which leads you up metal steps on to the viaduct. **Turn left and walk over the viaduct**; stay on the track, passing the old Coanwood platform. Cross the road into a car park and follow a sign for *Featherstone Rowfoot 1*. The track leads back to the car park at the start.

FEATHERSTONE CASTLE

Appendix

Tourist Information Centres

Alnwick	T: 01670 622 152
Berwick-upon-Tweed	T: 01670 622 155
Corbridge	T: 01434 632 815
Craster	T: 01665 576 007
Druridge Bay	T: 01670 760 968
Haltwhistle	T: 01434 321 863
Hauxley Wildlife Discovery Centre	T: 01665 568 324
Haydon Bridge	T: 01434 688 658
Hexham	T: 01670 620 450
Kielder Castle	T: 01434 250 209
Morpeth	T: 01670 623 455
Rothbury	T: 01670 622 151
Seahouses	T: 01670 625 593
South Tynedale Railway	T: 01434 338 214
The Sill	T: 01434 341 200
Walltown	T: 01434 344 396
Wooler	T: 01668 282 123

Food & Drink

Cafes

Blacksmiths Coffee Shop, Belsay	T: 01661 881 024
Bolam Lake Cafe	T: 01661 881 234
Carriages Tea Room, Bellingham	T: 01434 221 151
Ingram Cafe, Ingram	T: 01665 578 100
Kielder Castle Cafe, Kielder	T: 01434 250 100
Shoreline Cafe, Craster	T: 01665 571 251
The Barn at Beal, Beal	T: 01289 540 044
The Running Fox, Longframlington	T: 01665 570 760

Pubs

Holly Bush Inn, Greenhaugh	T: 01434 240 391
Rose & Thistle, Alwinton	T: 01669 650 226
The Anglers Arms, Kielder	T: 01434 250 072
The Bamburgh Castle Inn, Seahouses	T: 01665 720 283
The Castle Inn, Bamburgh	T: 01668 214 616
The Dirty Bottles, Alnwick	T: 01665 606 193
The Golden Lion, Allendale	T: 01434 683 225
The Greenhead Hotel, Greenhead	T: 01697 747 411
The Jolly Fisherman, Craster	T: 01665 576 461
The Kings Head, Allendale	T: 01434 683 681
The Masons Arms, Norham	T: 01289 382 326
The Ship Inn, Low Newton-by-the-Sea	T: 01665 576 262
The Star Inn, Harbottle	T: 01669 650 221
The Wallace Arms, Rowfoot	T: 01434 298 921
Twice Brewed Inn, Bardon Mill	T: 01434 344 534

Outdoor Shops

Go Outdoors, Berwick upon Tweed	T: 03443 876 757
Kielder Cycle Centre, Kielder	T: 01434 250 457
Millets, Hexham	T: 01434 693 606
Montane Outlet Store, Ashington	T: 01670 817 932
Mountain Warehouse, Morpeth	T: 01670 505 105
Otterburn Mill, Rothbury	T: 01669 622 814

Weather

www.metoffice.gov.uk

Accommodation
Hostels

YHA Youth Hostels can be found in the following places. For more information please visit
www.yha.org.uk

Alnwick	T: 03452 602 418
Bellingham	T: 03452 602 534
Berwick	T: 03453 719 676
Ninebanks	T: 03452 602 787
The Sill	T: 03452 602 702
Wooler	T: 03452 602 931

Bunkhouses

Allendale Bunkhouse, Allendale T: 01434 618 579
Barrowburn Camping Barn,
Harbottle T: 01669 650 059
Greenhead Bunkhouse,
Greenhead T: 01697 747 411
Mounthooly Bunkhouse,
College Valley T: 01668 216 210

Campsites

Kielder Village Campsite,
Kielder T: 01434 239 257

Useful Websites

Holy Island Crossing Times:
https://holyislandcrossingtimes.northumberland.gov.uk
www.discoverourland.co.uk
www.hadrianswallcountry.co.uk
www.northpennines.org.uk
www.northumberlandcoastaonb.org
www.northumberlandnationalpark.org.uk
www.visitnorthumberland.com

Other Publications

Hadrian's Wall Path Guidemap
Vertebrate Publishing **www.v-publishing.co.uk**

Day Walks in the North York Moors
Tony Harker, Vertebrate Publishing
www.v-publishing.co.uk

Day Walks in the Lake District
Stephen Goodwin, Vertebrate Publishing
www.v-publishing.co.uk

Day Walks in the Yorkshire Dales
Bernard Newman, Vertebrate Publishing
www.v-publishing.co.uk

Day Walks in the Peak District:
20 new circular routes
Norman Taylor & Barry Pope, Vertebrate Publishing
www.v-publishing.co.uk

Day Walks in the South Pennines
Paul Besley, Vertebrate Publishing
www.v-publishing.co.uk

Big Trails: Great Britain & Ireland
Edited by Kathy Rogers and Stephen Ross,
Vertebrate Publishing
www.v-publishing.co.uk

About the Author

David Wilson is a Northumberland Trail and Tour Guide and has spent his life exploring this remote and unique landscape. An ambassador for the county, he can be found in a variety of locations from the wilds of Northumberland National Park to trekking along Hadrian's Wall.

Alongside his passion for tourism in North East England, he is also a long-standing Ordnance Survey GetOutside Champion. This role sees him encouraging people to enjoy the outdoors safely and sustainably – the core principle of *Day Walks in Northumberland*, his first guidebook.

Vertebrate Publishing
At Vertebrate Publishing we publish books to inspire adventure.

It's our rule that the only books we publish are those that we'd want to read or use ourselves. We endeavour to bring you beautiful books that stand the test of time and that you'll be proud to have on your bookshelf for years to come.

The Peak District was the inspiration behind our first books. Our offices are situated on its doorstep, minutes away from world-class climbing, biking and hillwalking. We're driven by our own passion for the outdoors, for exploration, and for the natural world; it's this passion that we want to share with our readers.

We aim to inspire everyone to get out there. We want to connect readers – young and old – with the outdoors and the positive impact it can have on well-being. We think it's particularly important that young people get outside and explore the natural world, something we support through our publishing programme.

As well as publishing award-winning new books, we're working to make available many out-of-print classics in both print and digital formats. These are stories that we believe are unique and significant; we want to make sure that they continue to be shared and enjoyed.
www.v-publishing.co.uk

DAY WALKS GUIDEBOOKS

Written by local authors, each pocket-sized guidebook features:

- 20 great day-length walks
- Ordnance Survey 1:25,000-scale maps
- easy-to-follow directions
- distance & navigation information
- refreshment stops & local area information
- detailed appendix

1. **DAY WALKS IN THE CAIRNGORMS**
2. **DAY WALKS IN FORT WILLIAM & GLEN COE**
3. **DAY WALKS IN LOCH LOMOND & THE TROSSACHS**
4. **DAY WALKS IN SNOWDONIA**
5. **DAY WALKS IN THE BRECON BEACONS**
6. **DAY WALKS ON THE PEMBROKESHIRE COAST**
7. **DAY WALKS IN THE LAKE DISTRICT**
8. **DAY WALKS IN NORTHUMBERLAND**
9. **DAY WALKS IN THE YORKSHIRE DALES**
10. **DAYS WALKS IN THE NORTH YORK MOORS**
11. **DAY WALKS IN THE SOUTH PENNINES**
12. **DAY WALKS IN THE PEAK DISTRICT**
13. **DAY WALKS IN THE PEAK DISTRICT**
14. **DAY WALKS IN EAST ANGLIA**
15. **DAY WALKS IN THE COTSWOLDS**
16. **DAY WALKS IN DEVON**
17. **DAY WALKS ON THE HIGH WEALD**
18. **DAY WALKS ON THE SOUTH DOWNS**

Available from book shops or direct from **www.v-publishing.co.uk**